M.

Human Memory
and Knowledge

CONTRIBUTIONS IN LIBRARIANSHIP AND
INFORMATION SCIENCE

Series Editor: Paul Wasserman

Glynn Harmon

Human Memory
and Knowledge

A Systems Approach

Contributions in Librarianship and Information Science
Number 6

Greenwood Press
Westport, Connecticut o London, England

Library of Congress Cataloging in Publication Data

Harmon, Glynn.
    Human memory and knowledge.

    (Contributions in librarianship and information
science, no. 6)
    Bibliography: p.
    1. Memory. 2. Cognition. 3. System analysis.
I. Title. II. Series.
BF371.H37   001.53   72-809
ISBN 0-8371-6379-X

Library of Congress Catalog Card Number: 72-809

ISBN: 0-8371-6379-X

First published in 1973

Greenwood Press, a division of Williamhouse-Regency Inc.
51 Riverside Avenue, Westport, Connecticut 06880

Manufactured in the United States of America

Contents

List of Illustrations and Tables

Illustrations

Tables

Preface

Ever since the first humanoid stopped running for his life long enough to wonder what lay beyond the near horizon, man has been trying to make sense out of the chaos he lives in. Age after age has fashioned scheme after scheme, each proponent hoping that his will be the master, ultimate scheme. But all ages come to the same impasse. The horizon keeps moving back. Every answer poses a new question, until we have more knowledge than we know what to do with and we stand in peril of choking to death on a surplus of erudition.

At length it has become clear that there is no master scheme, but only schemes which serve for a time. One may be a single step from knowledge to wisdom, and another may lead in one of several directions. Often, instead of urging us toward the far distance, it turns us inward until we discover that it might not be the world that has baffled us so much, but the structure of our own minds. In this book I have tried to show that man-made schemes of knowledge bear man's indelible mental imprint.

By way of acknowledgment, I would like to thank the U. S. Office of Education for financial support rendered under the auspices of Case Western Reserve University, and to the University of Denver for financial assistance during preparation of the manuscript. I am particularly indebted to Dr. William Goffman for his stimulating encouragement throughout my inquiry, and to Dr. Conrad H. Rawski who in 1964 sparked my interest in epistemology. I wish also to thank the editors of the American Society for Information Science for their permission to include in chapter 5 an expanded version of my earlier paper "On the Evolution of Information Science," *Journal of American Society for Information Science* 22 (July/August 1971): 235-241.

Human Memory
and Knowledge

1

Introduction

This inquiry explores the relationship between human memory limitations and the formation of various fields of systematic knowledge. Because all existing fields of recorded human knowledge can be viewed as products of human cognitive operations, the question arises as to how human cognitive efforts and constraints have influenced the formation and structure of these various fields. This inquiry compares the formation of a limited number of sub-disciplines, disciplines, and interdisciplinary fields. Special emphasis is given to the rise and development of information science, the focal discipline of the study.

The Problem

The central problem of the inquiry is the extent to which fields of recorded knowledge, particularly information science, have been formed, structured, and circumscribed in accordance with the necessities and constraints imposed by a relatively constant and limited span of human memory. The possible existence of a strong relationship between human memory limits and the organization of knowledge could serve to explain or predict the rise and maturity of various disciplines.

Briefly, the genesis of the problem might be interpreted as a complex of events which originated with limited human memory capacity. Historically, man's limited, innate memory capacity gave rise to his use of records. The accumulation of recorded knowledge soon exceeded the capacity of individual memories and forced individuals to specialize. Specialization gave rise to telescopic inquiry, the subsequent fragmentation of knowledge, and the need for interdisciplinary communication. The following paragraphs elaborate on this simplified interpretation of the problem.

J. H. Shera, a noted historian on the subject of recorded knowledge, summarizes the conditions which gave rise to the need for memoranda or records.

> . . . oral communication was severely limited by the temporal boundaries of human memory and the spatial parameters of human contact. Even though man could communicate . . . one break in the chain and the idea was lost—perhaps forever. Mnemonic devices, such as rhyme were invented to assist in the preservation of this chain, but at best they were imperfectly effective. . . . man discovered that it was possible, by means of some form of graphic record, to transcend space and time to become independent of human memory and contact.[1]

The sum of accumulated, recorded knowledge probably exceeded the grasp of most individuals well before 1600 A.D. Colin Cherry estimates that Leibniz (1646-1716) was probably mankind's last truly well-informed generalist.[2] This estimate might be fairly accurate, as it was during this era that groups of encyclopedists began to compile grand syntheses of human knowledge to bridge the gulfs between areas of specialized inquiry.[3] Teams of scientific investigators, united by the necessity of specialization as well as by common interests, began to form. Early teamwork is marked by the founding of the first "invisible college" of informal scientific collaborators in 1660—the Royal Society of London.[4]

According to Matson, restrictive specialization began essentially with the adoption of the mechanistic view which arose from Newtonian physics; man's unified image of experience was fractured into specialized domains of inquiry—the sciences and the humanities.[5] Royce cogently argues that the human mind and spirit have been seriously and chronically crippled by a process of encapsulation, or highly restrictive specialization. But we can also look at encapsulation as a natural concomitant of human cognitive limitations. Man does not hear sounds outside the range of 20 to 20,000 cycles per second, nor does he respond to more than approximately 1/70 of the total light spectrum. He is further limited in the exercise of his imagination, the rationality and abstractness of his thought, and, as Royce argues, "memories are rarely prodigious."[6]

P. W. Bridgman has also emphasized the effects of human cognitive limits.

> . . . it is impossible to transcend the human reference point . . . the structure of nature may eventually be such that our processes of thought do not correspond to it sufficiently to permit us to think about it at all. . . . We are now approaching a bound beyond which we are forever estopped from pushing our inquiries, not by the construc-

tion of the world but by the construction of our-
selves.[7]

Contemporary scientific laws, Schlesinger argues, are
biased because they represent only those aspects of
nature which are sufficiently simple for the human
mind to manage.[8] In his work *Science Is Not Enough*,
Vannevar Bush views the problem of partiality or
incompleteness as one which pervades contemporary
science.[9] Weinberg discusses the "well-recognized fragmentation" of science and expresses the fear that the
departments of science could cease to communicate
and fertilize each other.[10] Boulding states:

> One wonders sometimes if science will not grind
> to a stop in an assemblage of walled-in hermits,
> each mumbling to himself words in a private lan-
> guage that only he can understand. . . . The
> spread of specialized deafness means that some-
> one who ought to know something that someone
> else knows isn't able to find it out for lack of
> generalized ears.[11]

So far, through the above trial of testimony, the
restrictive impact of human memory limits has been
emphasized and its impact reviewed in terms of the
necessity for recorded knowledge, the subsequent
specialization of inquiry, and the mutual alienation of
the departments of knowledge. Several selected studies
emphasize the relationship between human memory
limits, concept formation, and the evolution of disciplinary systems of knowledge.

In 1945 Vannevar Bush pioneered the concept of
a "memex," an information storage and retrieval

device designed to augment the memory capacity of its individual users. More recently, Bush has stated that the fundamental problem involved in the design of the memex is to develop "moderately rapid access to a really large memory storage."[12] In his last work, *The Computer and the Brain,* John von Neuman addressed himself to the problem of providing high-capacity, rapid-access computer memory storage to augment natural or human memory capability.[13]

G. A. Miller published a classic article on the limits of human capacity for processing information.[14] The major points of his article are excerpted below.

1. The mean span of absolute judgment is 2.6 bits with a standard deviation of 0.6 bit. In terms of distinguishable alternatives, this mean corresponds to about 6.5 categories, one standard deviation includes 5 to 10 categories, and the total range is from 3 to 15 categories. . . .

2. There seems to be some limitation built into us either by learning or by the design of our nervous systems, a limit that keeps our channel capacities in this general range. . . . this capacity does not vary a great deal from one simple sensory attribute to another.

3. There is a finite span of immediate memory and for a lot of different kinds of test materials this span is about seven items in length. . . . With binary items the span is about nine, although it drops to about five with monosyllabic English words. . . . Absolute judgment is limited by the amount of information. Immediate memory is limited by the number of items. . . .

4. Since the memory span is a fixed number of chunks we can increase the number of bits of information that it contains simply by building larger and larger chunks, each chunk containing more information than before.
5. The span of absolute judgment and the span of immediate memory impose severe limitations on the amount of information that we are able to receive, process and remember.

In a similar vein Simon and Newell point out that in contrast to long-term memory, which is essentially unlimited in capacity, short-term memory is indeed small. Very little of the total amount of material in the long-term memory can be recalled or processed during the performance of any particular task. That is, while the total content of memory is potentially implicated in a cognitive task, only a minute fraction of the total is actually implicated in the task. When the contents of memory are not processed in a complex manner, the short-term memory under some conditions appears to hold Miller's famous seven chunks. Simon and Newell conclude that concept formation is continuously dependent on the structure and content of memory.[15]

The relation between memory and concept formation appears to be a particularly important factor in the formation of systematic knowledge. Victor Yngve has proposed that English sentences, and probably those of other languages, tend to have a length and depth that does not exceed the seven plus-or-minus two span of immediate memory. In addition, many ingenious linguistic innovations are designed to circumvent the limitations of human memory.[16] Thus memory limits do appear to influence the construction of sentences, which can be viewed as rather basic building blocks essential to the formation of more elaborate networks. Reitman employs a human information processing and set theory approach to concept formation, treating the "whole problem of cognitive structure as a matter of sets of cognitive elements interconnected together in complex networks."[17] Given a sufficient number of cognitive elements and an adequate set defining criterion (rule or hypothesis) the formation of an ordered cognitive set or concept becomes more probable.

Kelly's classic theory of personal constructs explains concept formation as a process involving the organization of constructs into a complex hierarchical network, or a construct system. Such constructs possess *limited ranges of convenience.* An individual cannot "stretch" his constructs too far beyond relatively convenient application.[18] Kelly's range of cognitive convenience appears to hold special significance in the study of the growth of science. Capek observes that "Euclidian Geometry, Newtonian Mechanics and Laplacean Determinism represented our intellectual adjustment to a *certain segment of reality,* and not to reality in its whole extent."[19] Niels Bohr expresses this view.

The main point to realize is that all knowledge presents itself within a conceptual framework adapted to account for previous experience and that any such frame may prove too narrow to comprehend new experiences. . . . the widening of the conceptual framework not only has served to restore order within the respective branches of knowledge, but has also disclosed analogies in our position with respect to analysis and synthesis of experience in apparently separated domains of knowledge, suggesting the possibility of an ever more embracing objective description.[20]

Simon presents a similar view but uses a systems approach to the formation of complex systems of knowledge. Such knowledge or disciplinary systems evolve gradually through the combination of stable subassemblies into hierarchical forms. "Subsystems will form until all the capacity for strong interaction is utilized in their construction. Then these subsystems will be linked by the weaker second order bonds into larger systems."[21] Simon notes that the formation of large systems depends on stable subassemblies.

In general, then, the individual studies reviewed in this section do not directly indicate a definite relationship between the three parameters of memory, concept formation, and the formations of disciplinary systems. Collectively, however, these studies might at least suggest such a relationship, and this will be explored. In this study the growth of disciplinary systems is viewed largely as a function of concept formation which, in turn, may be seen as an application of memory. Human memory limits appear to be relatively narrow and fixed; they could thus possibly serve to restrict man-made concepts and disciplinary systems to narrowly circumscribed configurations. Before elaborating on the above discussion, it is necessary to clarify the meaning of a few key terms, to state the chief objectives and hypotheses, and to explain the method and limitations of this investigation.

Definitions[22]

Suprasystem—A relatively complete, comprehensive system made up of subordinate systems. In this study suprasystem generally refers to a potentially emerging encyclopedic system of man's knowledge.

System—A set of elements standing in interaction. In this study, the term system is frequently synonymous with *discipline* (i.e., existing disciplines, such as physics or chemistry).

Subsystem—An element or functional component of a larger system which fulfills the conditions of a system in itself but which also plays a specialized role in the operation of the larger system; a subdiscipline or subfield, such as mechanics, or electricity.

Component—A part of a subsystem; specifically a major concept or discovery; a sub-subsystem.

Formation—Integration, organization, or synthesis of smaller systems parts of systems into relatively discrete wholes.

Differentiation—A process whereby parts of a system become distinguishable from one another and relatively specialized.

Short-term memory—The immediate memory span involved in episodes during which the entire cycle of sensing, retaining and processing information occupies a few seconds. In contrast, long-term memory is applied to the retention and use of learned information which is mobilized after a longer time lapse.

Objectives and Hypotheses

The general purpose of this study is to explore the relationship between human short-term memory limits and the formation of disciplinary systems. More specifically, the study represents an attempt to describe chronologically the key events and processes involved in the formation of a number of disciplinary subsystems, systems, and interdisciplinary systems. Further, it attempts to estimate and project the growth rates of such systems and to discuss the possible formation of a suprasystem—a systematic, grand coalition of man's knowledge.

In accordance with these objectives, a few general hypotheses may now be stated. First, it might be expected that a scientist, when following a particular line of inquiry, would tend to periodically synthesize his findings or those of his predecessors into cognitively convenient configurations. Hence, human systems of knowledge will tend to consist of highly circumscribed organizations—those which lend themselves to easy human information processing by being restricted in scope.

A second hypothesis, somewhat more self-evident, is that the formation of larger systems of knowledge from smaller systems is possible after a requisite number of smaller systems or ideas are available for synthesis. This notion corresponds with the notion in mathematical set theory that, for other than a null or empty set, a minimum number of elements is needed to compose an ordered set.

Third, the formation of knowledge systems tends to occur before the available number of smaller systems or ideas exceeds the limits of human short-term memory. As the available number of separate smaller systems approaches the seven-plus-or-minus-two limit of human short term memory, these smaller systems must be combined into a larger system so that a scientist can keep track of them. Inquiry becomes too difficult or unprofitable without the needed systematization.

Fourth, if a necessary synthesis is not done by one individual or group, it will tend to be done by a different individual or group. This hypothesis relates to the frequently occurring scientific phenomenon of multiple, simultaneous discovery. Two or more scientists will tend to make the same discovery at about the same time.

Fifth, it can be hypothesized that a basic pattern underlying the formation of systematic knowledge is one of synthesis. Subsystems or subdisciplines will tend to form when a small number of complementary ideas is available. In accordance with the preceding hypothesis that human short-term memory will influence such formative patterns, approximately seven ideas or contributions are required for the synthesis of a subsystem. Extending these notions, systems or disciplines would tend to form when approximately seven complementary subsystems or subdisciplines are available. It is further proposed that larger supradisciplinary organizations of knowledge will tend to consist of approximately seven systems. These seven-member supradisciplinary systems might consist of such general areas of human knowledge as the humanities, the physical, biological or social sciences, or comprehensive classification systems.

The above general hypotheses, then, have guided this investigation. At this point the basic notions are kept simple, not to deny or escape the complexities of systematic knowledge accumulation, but to state the case with a greater degree of clarity than would otherwise be possible. Attention is given to these complexities, however, particularly to such phenomena as the formation of hybrid and interdisciplinary systems, which might be viewed as responses to the inadequacies inherent in isolated disciplinary systems. Also discussed is the potential emergence of a suprasystem of knowledge—a totally integrated and comprehensive system of human knowledge that might emerge at some future time. Particular attention is given to information science as a potential catalyst in the formation of a suprasystem of human knowledge.

Remarks on Method

This inquiry employs an historical, systems analytic approach in which the chronological evolution of several disciplinary systems is traced by starting with relatively small systems and proceeding to successively larger systems. The concepts of general systems theory are used to clarify relationships involved in the evolution of systems.

During the early phases of this inquiry, it proved to be relatively unprofitable to analyze single systems as separate entities. Each system has its predecessors, successors, competitors, and collaborators. The study of a given system as an isolated entity can reduce the perspective required to locate the system in its wider disciplinary context. Therefore, this inquiry is not restricted to one or two cases, or to a short historical interval. The analysis is holistic in order to trace the diachronic evolution of systems over several centuries. Particular eras are, however, treated in order to assess the synchronic significance of certain phenomena, such as the relatively simultaneous, independent emergence of highly similar miniature subsystems (discoveries) or larger systems (disciplines).

With respect to sampling problems, which specific systems should be selected from the entire population of systems? The potentially infinite scope of this inquiry, as well as the obvious possibility of biased sampling procedures, pose two particularly serious sampling problems. Because information science is taken as a focal discipline of the study, analysis of those systems which contributed to the development of information science can be revealing. These contributory systems include mathematics, logic, linguistics, psychology, systems theory, and others. The study of contemporary interdisciplinary systems which—like information science—are communications-oriented, can also serve to reveal the disciplinary status of information science and to limit the sampling possibilities. Therefore, samples are drawn from groups of contributory and interdisciplinary systems apparently related to information science. Specifically, major features of the evolution of mathematics, a rational discipline, are analyzed. Additional cases are drawn from the empirical sciences, particularly physics.

In order to reduce the possibility of a biased sampling procedure, and to assure adequate replicability of the investigation, additional controls are introduced. Because of the difficulty in designating precisely which relationships and events were basic to the formation of systems in the selected subjects during different eras, the judgments and consensus of at least two historians are employed to designate important relationships and events. At least two historians must agree, for example, on what constitutes a "landmark" event in the formation of a given system. In this way, by using the judgments of the same historians, someone else should be able to replicate this investigation.

In general, the initial publication dates of first works which announce key events, such as a discovery, are used to represent the dates of such discoveries. If, however, a key event is not announced through publication within five years from the actual date of that key event, then the actual date of the event (as noted by at least two historians) is used rather than the date of publication. This procedure is used because, in a few cases, the publication of the discovery was inordinately delayed. The occurrence of some events, such as the emergence of a discipline, is often difficult to date. Therefore, the dates of key publications by "founding fathers" or key figures are used to mark chronologically nebulous events.

All of the hypotheses which relate to the temporal and formative patterns of all systems are tested throughout the investigation by means of an analysis of developmental patterns of various subsystems and systems. Data consist primarily of time intervals (expressed in years) between key events. A method is developed to predict key disciplinary syntheses and to analyze their subsequent changes in form. In addition, specific chapters are devoted to the notion that seven component ideas or systems are merged periodically into successively larger systems. Following this introduction, chapter 2 traces the chronological formation of several subsystems in mathematics and physics. Major events which culminate in the formation of each subsystem are recorded and compared. Chapter 3 analyzes the formative and developmental patterns of systems in the mathematical, physical, biological, and social sciences, as well as the development of hybrid and interdisciplinary systems. Chapter 4 explores divisions of the entire circle of man's knowledge from ancient to modern times and discusses the world encyclopedia concept. The humanities, and the physical, biological, social, and communication sciences are viewed as sub-suprasystems of a potentially emergent suprasystem of knowledge. Chapter 5 applies the findings of previous chapters in an analysis of the development of information science as a disciplinary system and discusses the future development of information science.

Finally, a few limitations of this inquiry must be stated. The priorities and mode of investigation used in this study serve to restrict its scope. First, the study is not intended to serve as a definitive treatise on the growth, philosophy, or history of knowledge. Because the relatively new approach of systems analysis is employed, it is best to think of this as an exploratory study rather than a definitive one.

Second, the study is basically a macro-analysis rather than a micro-analysis. It concentrates on the gross, aggregate features involved in the formation of systems. Highly detailed analyses of singular events are sacrificed in the hope that a frontal attack on the problem will yield more information than a narrowly circumscribed study limited to one or two cases within a compressed time interval. Consequently, a "landmark" level of generality is maintained throughout the study. The highest degree of specificity employed relates to the factor of short-term memory.

Third, the study deals with disciplinary systems in a general way and is restricted to basic, rather than technological or applied, disciplines. Information science is the only discipline discussed in detail. Further, the similarities rather than the differences of system formation have been stressed in order to develop a method of predicting system formations. Other limitations are treated throughout the book.

2

Formation of Subsystems

In this chapter, the manner in which several major concepts were conceived in both rational and empirical disciplines is analyzed. The chapter focuses on the influence of human memory limitations on the synthetic and systematic aspects of concept formation. Those concepts which have developed into major components of disciplinary systems are treated as subsystems. In turn, key ideas used in the formation of subsystems are generally treated as subsystems.

First, the nature of subsystem formation is explored by tracing the chronological development of several cases in mathematics and physics. Second, these chronological developments are analyzed and a method is suggested for estimating the time intervals required for subsystem formation. Third, the method is applied to two cases to determine the extent to which their formation might have been predicted. Fourth, relationships between the formation of subsystems and memory limitations are discussed in order to assess the role which human memory plays in the systematic accumulation of ideas.

Nature and Chronologies of Subsystem Formation

The chronological order of several subsystem formations in mathematics and the empirical sciences can be recorded. As Sarton points out, chronological reconstructions of very complex phenomena are highly oversimplified because they neatly depict direct progressions of events which culminate in major syntheses. Genuine scientific progress is probably seldom a direct progression from point *A* to point *B*; it involves, rather, a time consuming, trial and error series of efforts resulting in frequent digressions, retrogressions and progressions.[1] Further, there is no guarantee that such reconstructions are historically accurate. The possibility of historical falsification or distortion and biased sampling is always present. To repeat, control for such possibilities is provided by using the consensus of at least two historians to designate precisely which events were basic to the formation of a subsystem in cases where an autobiographical account of a discovery is not employed.

The use of landmark events to depict the underlying evolution of a disciplinary system is possibly analogous to charting a series of floating icebergs. Only a small portion of each iceberg protrudes above the water's surface, while its major portion remains submerged. The superficial portion of the iceberg provides only an approximate indication of its full dimensions or true center of gravity. A single iceberg can have more than one protuberance—a case analogous to multiple scientific discovery or other duplicate scientific activity. Landmark events, by their nature and occurrence, suggest the underlying development of a disciplinary system.

Euclidian Geometry

Euclidian geometry provides a relatively early case of subsystem formation. It is reasonably well established that Euclid's work is a systematic synthesis of prior contributions. The views of Sarton and Bell are quoted respectively:

> The way for Euclidean mathematics was very gradually and thoroughly prepared . . . by three centuries of persistent investigations. . . . The historian is made to witness the building up, as it were stone by stone, of that wonderful monument, geometry, as it was finally transmitted to us in the *Elements*.[2]
>
> For the first time in history masses of isolated discoveries were unified and correlated by a single guiding principle, that of rigorous deduction from explicitly stated assumptions. Some of the Pythagoreans and Eudoxus before Euclid had executed details of the grand design, but it remained for Euclid to see it all and see it whole.[3]

An estimate of which prior contributions were most systematically significant in Euclid's synthesis can be made by comparing the judgments of different historians. Smith's relatively detailed *History of Mathematics* discusses the contributions of at least twenty individuals, but most of these contributions were either dwarfed or subsumed by more major contributions. The historical accounts of Ball and Struik specifically indicate, in agreement with Smith, that Thales, Pythagoras, Hippocrates of Chios, Archytas, Theaetetus, Plato, and Eudoxus made significant contributions.[4] Smith and Ball agree that Oenopides of Chios made a significant pre-Euclidean contribution but Struik's account omits Oenopides. The following chronology of these nine contributions shows approximate dates (B.C.), the names of contributors and the books of Euclid's *Elements* which incorporated their contributions.[5]

600	Thales	I, III, VI
540	Pythagoras	I, II, VI, XI
465	Oenopides	I
460	Hippocrates	I, III, XII
400	Archytas	III, XI
380	Plato	Foundations and method
375	Theaetetus	X
370	Eudoxus	I, V, X, XII, XIII
300	Euclid	*Elements* I to XIII

It is interesting to note that the chronology of formation extends 300 years, in contrast to the compressed chronologies of more recent eras, which are discussed later. Further, the contributions of several men were prerequisite to the construction of a viable system of geometry which could stand, essentially intact, for over 2,200 years. It remained, of course, for Euclid's successors to refine, extend and challenge his system.

Calculus

The second case of disciplinary subsystem formation to be considered is Newton's discovery of the calculus. Struik argues that the calculus could only be discovered by men who understood the geometrical methods of the Greeks and of Cavalieri, as well as the algebraic methods of Descartes and Wallis. "Such men could have appeared only after 1660, and they did actually appear in Newton and Leibniz."[6] The relatively simultaneous, independent discovery of the calculus by Newton, Leibniz and Seki Kōwa suggested that such a synthesis was not only possible, after the requisite concepts and methods were available, but also necessary. Further progress in mathematics and science depended heavily on the calculus.

Newton discovered the calculus first (Newton in 1666; Leibniz in 1676), but Leipniz published it first (Leibniz 1684-1686; Newton 1704-1736).[7] Smith reports that Seki Kōwa, the "Newton" of Japan, had probably invented the calculus which appeared in Japan around 1680.[8] In any case, the invention of calculus was possible through a synthesis of the existing systems of plane geometry, algebra, trigonometry, analytic geometry, and irrational numbers.[9] Simon emphasizes that the availability of viable, simple systems supports the relatively rapid formation of more complex systems. He views system formation as a process analogous to biological evolution in which ontogeny recapitulates phylogeny. "In most subjects . . . the progress from elementary to advanced courses is to a considerable extent a progress through the conceptual history of the science itself."[10] However, Simon adds, such a recapitulation is seldom literal.

In formulating his first tract on calculus, (October 1666), Newton depended directly and chiefly on the systematic works of Descartes, Hudde, Wallis, Heuraet, and Barrow. The compiler and editor of Newton's mathematical papers, D. T. Whiteside, has constructed a schematic diagram of the discovery, which is reproduced in Figure 1.[11]

While the schematic reconstruction of Newton's discovery doubtlessly oversimplifies the actual event, it perhaps approximates several authentic relationships between short term memory span, concept formation

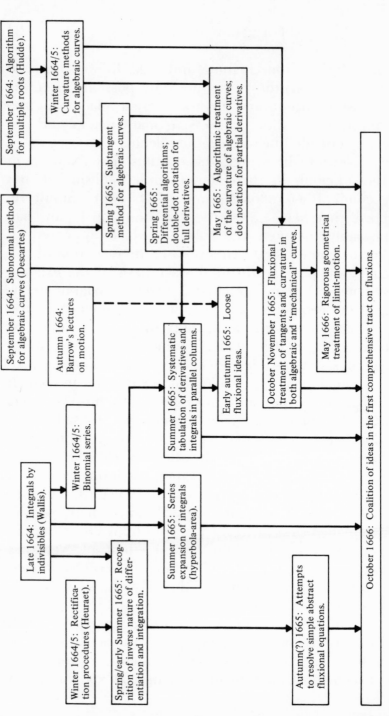

Figure 1.—Coalition of Newton's Ideas on the Calculus (Fluxions)

and the development of systematic knowledge. Apparently, relatively few figures—Heuraet, Wallis, Barrow, Descartes and Hudde—had a direct, precipitating influence in the final phase of Newton's discovery. According to Whiteside, however, Newton was also heavily subject to the long-run, predisposing influences of Euclid, Archimedes, Oughtred, Viète and others. Such predisposing influences would presumably have been active as components of Newton's long term memory. The schematic reconstruction also illustrates the process of concept formation, revealing Newton's ability to "go beyond" the available information.[12] The resulting concept or system formation consists of a coalition of six components, according to the schematic reconstruction. Further, the greatest number of fundamental steps in the sequence from beginning to end is held to six, illustrating the possible effects of short term memory limits on the length of a syllogistic chain. Poincaré discusses the dependence of mathematical reasoning on memory.

> Between the moment in which we first meet a proposition as conclusion of one syllogism and that in which we reencounter it as a premise of another syllogism, occasionally some time will elapse . . . so it may happen that we have forgotten it. . . .
> Often the mathematician uses a rule. . . . But subsequently he trusts his memory and afterward only applies it in a mechanical way; and then if his memory fails him, he may apply it all wrong. According to this, the special aptitude for mathematics would be due only to a very sure memory or to a prodigious force of attention.[13]

Additional features of Newton's discovery are indicative of the relationship between memory span and concept formation, and can be noted in the text of his October, 1666 tract.[14] First, each of Newton's main demonstrations or proofs were limited to a maximum of five syllogisms. Of nine proofs, the average number of syllogisms per proof is 3.44, while the median is 4. Second, these syllogisms consist of four to eleven terms. The average number of terms per syllogism is 5.78 and the median is 6.83. Third, the number of points which Newton labeled in all forty-four geometrical drawings, for use in his demonstrations, ranged between three and seventeen. The average number of labeled points per illustration is 8.25 and the median is 7.90.

In summary, Newton's initial conceptualization of the calculus involved the processing of approximately five or six systematic ideas. He used approximately three or four syllogisms per proof, six terms per syllogism, and eight reference points per illustration, thus staying within the seven to nine upper limit number of short term memory. The final discovery was apparently a gradual synthesis of elements into a cognitively manageable whole.

In order to establish a chronology for the formation of calculus as a subsystem of mathematics, one might use the dates of works which Newton relied upon directly to make his discovery. However, sole use of this procedure would be somewhat unrealistic in tracing the evolution of systematic knowledge because Newton's direct sources were extensions and refinements of earlier pioneer works in algebra, geometry, and other mathematical areas. The following chronology is based primarily on the criterion of the time at which the requisite mathematical components were available to support the invention of calculus, whether by Newton or someone else. The chronology represents key developments leading to the calculus, according to Smith, Struik and Boyer.[15]

1591	Viète	*Isagoge* and other works on algebra and trigo-nometry. Improved by Harriet and Oughtred.
1609	Kepler	*Astronomia nova*. Crude integral calculus.
1635	Cavalieri	*Geometria indivisibilibus* and later work. Simple form of calculus.
1637	Descartes	*Discours de la méthode* Appendix: *La géométria*. United algebra and geometry. Developed further by Fermat.
1655	Wallis	*Arithmetica infinitorum*. Extended algebra to analysis. Similar work by Huygens.
1658	Hudde	Maxima and minima of Fermat generalized.
1663	Barrow	Differential methods. Published *Lectiones geometriae*, 1670. Similar work by Pascal.
1666	Newton	First tract on calculus.
1684	Leibniz	First paper on calculus.

Universal Gravitation

According to Caws, Newton's work in Mechanics was essentially a synthesis or cluster of previous major contributions.[16] According to Cajori and More, the following series of contributions was essential to Newton's synthesis.[17]

1543	Copernicus	*De revolutionibus*
1588	Brahe	*Epistolarium astronomicarum libri*
1609	Kepler	*Astronomia nova*
1632	Galileo	*Dialogues on the Two New Sciences*
1637	Descartes	*Discours de la méthode*
1645	Bullialdi	*Astronomia philolaica*
1670	Barrow	*Lectiones geometriae*
1673	Huygens	*Horologrum oscillatorium*
1687	Newton	*Principia*

Unified Geometry

Felix Klein demonstrated in 1872 that Riemann's elliptic geometry, with Euclid's parabolic geometry and Lobachevsky's hyperbolic geometry, were particular instances of a more general geometry. Thus, according to Bell, Klein's synthesis terminated the formal conflict between these geometries.[18] A chronology of this development follows:[19]

1733   Saccheri *Euclides ab omni naevo vindicatus* (Euclid Freed of Every Flaw). Forerunner of non-Euclidean Geometry.

1770   Lambert *Die Theorie der Parallellinien* (posthumous, 1786). Attempted non-Euclidian Geometry.

1794   Legendre *Eléments de géométrie*. Elliptic functions and other contributions.

1820   Gauss indirectly encouraged Bolyai and Lobachevsky to formulate non-Euclidean geometry.

1829   Lobachevsky "Principles of Geometry" in *Kazan Messenger*. Bolyai *Tentamen*. Simultaneous discovery of non-Euclidian geometry.

1844 Grassmann *Ausdehnungslehre*. Theory of extension.

1854 Riemann *Habilitationschrift*. Generalized Geometry.

1872 Klein Erlanger Program—Synthesis and codification of geometry.

Nobel Awards

Insofar as Euclidian geometry, the calculus and Newtonian mechanics at one time monopolized mathematical or physical thought, these subsystems might have been assigned disciplinary status. Very similar formations provided the basis for entire disciplinary systems. For example, Hutton's *Theory of the Earth* (1785) served as a viable basis for the development of geology; Lavoisier's work in chemistry won him acclaim as the "father of modern chemistry."[20] Thus the assignment of subsystem, system or other status to a given system might be largely a function of the relative degree of dominance of that system at the time. Today's system could be yesterday's subsystem, or conversely.

Excerpts from Nobel Award acceptance addresses reveal a similar mode of system formation, even though such cases might be regarded as subsubsystems of physics. A portion of Owen W. Richardson's Nobel Lecture reveals the major events which led to his laws of thermionic phenomena.

In 1873 Guthrie showed that a red-hot iron ball in air could retain a negative but not a positive charge. In a series of researches extending from 1882 to 1889, Elster and Geitel examined the charge collected on an insulated plate placed near various hot wires in diverse gases at different pressures. The observed effects were very specific and varied, but there emerged a general tendency for the plate to acquire a positive charge at low temperatures and high pressures, and a negative charge at high temperatures and low pressures. The matter became really interesting in 1899 when J. J. Thompson showed that the discharge from an incandescent carbon filament in a vacuum tube was carried by negative electrons. In 1900 McClelland showed that the currents from a negatively charged platinum wire were influenced very little, if at all, by changes in the nature and pressure of the surrounding gas, if the pressure were fairly low. These facts seemed to me to be highly significant, and I resolved to investigate the phenomenon thoroughly. . . . Theories of metallic conduction had been put forward between 1888 and 1900 by Thompson, Riecke and Drude.[21]

Richardson published his discovery in 1916 and was awarded the Nobel Prize in Physics in 1928. Richardson's account illustrates how a small number of facts served as a basis for the subsequent formation of a systematic explanation of thermionic phenomena. In summary, it might be seen that the formations of sub-subsystems, subsystems or systems are similar processes.

The mere availability of a number of facts or ideas, however, does not necessarily mean that they will be automatically organized. For example, Wolf-gang Pauli states that he had been strongly influenced in formulating his discovery by the concepts of Ryd-berg (1890), Zeeman (1896), Bohr (1913), Som-merfield (1916), and Landé (1921). In spite of the availability of these concepts, his results were inconclu-sive.

> At this time (1924) a paper of the English physi-cist, Stoner, appeared which contained . . . the fol-lowing essential remark: For a given value of the principle quantum number is the number of energy levels of a single electron in the alkali metal spectra in an external magnetic field the same as the number of electrons in the closed shell of the rare gases which corresponds to this principle quantum number.
>
> On the basis of my earlier results on the clas-sification of spectral terms in a strong magnetic field the general formulation of the exclusion principle became clear to me.[22]

Thus in 1925 Pauli was able to state his exclusion prin-ciple upon being exposed to a concept which com-plemented and organized the set of informational ele-ments already in his possession.

Duration of Subsystem Formation

Six cases of subsystem formation have been reviewed thus far. These cases will now be used to devise a formula to aid in the prediction of discoveries. It may be recalled that each case involved the synthesis of a limited number of contributions into a concept or subsystem of relatively general scope. The time required for the formation of each subsystem involved an interval of sustained inquiry extending from the date of the first contribution in the series to the date of synthesis or discovery. Hence, in each case this time span may be taken to represent 100 percent of the time involved, and all of the intermediate dates may be represented as fractions or percentages of the total time span. The six cases are summarized in Table 1; for each case the year of each event is followed by its percentage position in the total time span. It is interesting to note that from case to case each event is distributed in a rather similar and predictable fashion along the chronological scale.[23]

TABLE 1

ANALYSIS OF TIME INTERVALS IN SUBSYSTEM FORMATION

	Euclidian Geometry		Calculus		Gravitation	
	Year (B.C.)	Percent	Year	Percent	Year	Percent
1	600	0	1591	0	1543	0
2	540	20	1609	21	1588	31
3	465	45	1635	52	1609	46
4	460	47	1637	54	1632	62
5	400	67	1655	76	1637	65
6	380	73	1658	80	1645	71
7	375	75	1663	87	1670	88
8	370	77	1675	100	1673	94
9	300	100			1687	100

	Unified Geometry		Thermionic Emission		Exclusion Principle	
	Year	Percent	Year	Percent	Year	Percent
1	1773	0	1873	0	1890	0
2	1770	27	1885	28	1896	17
3	1794	44	1894	49	1913	66
4	1820	63	1899	60	1916	74
5	1829	69	1900	63	1921	88
6	1844	80	1916	100	1924	97
7	1854	87			1925	100
8	1872	100				

From Table 1, the average percentage position of each event in the series, with its total time span coefficient can be calculated. Each coefficient, it will be seen, may be used to predict the date of discovery.

Event	Mean Percent	Coefficient
1	0	0
2	24	4.17
3	50	2.00
4	60	1.67
5	71	1.41
6	83	1.20
7	87	1.15
8	94	1.06

Thus, the total time required for the formation of a given subsystem should be approximately 4.17 times the interval between the first and second events, twice the time interval between the first and third events, 1.67 times the interval between the first and fourth events and so on. The following formula includes these coefficients and provides for the averaging of successive estimates.

$$T = \frac{4.17\,a + 2.0\,b + 1.67\,c + 1.41\,d + 1.2\,e}{n}$$

where T = total time interval, expressed in years;

    a = years between events 1 and 2;

    b = years between events 1 and 3;

    c = years between events 1 and 4;

    d = years between events 1 and 5; etc.

    n = number of coefficients in the series, other than zero.

On the assumption that an alert, informed observer could recognize and evaluate key events along the same line of inquiry, as apparently many scientists have done, it should be possible to predict the approximate date of a major discovery or synthesis. This formula may now be tested by applying it to the chronologies which follow. A simplified history of genetics, constructed by Garrett Hardin, is reproduced below.[24]

Prehistory to 1908	Reign of the blending theory of inheritance.
1866	Publication of Mendel's theory of particulate theory of inheritance; unnoticed by scientific world.
1900	Rediscovery of Mendel's paper, and independent discovery of Mendelian genetics by De Vries, Correns, and Tschermak.
1908	Groundwork of population genetics laid independently by Hardy and Weinberg.
1900-*ca.* 1950	Thorough development of Mendelian genetics and cytogenetics; beginnings of biochemical genetics
1930	Implications of particulate theory made clear by Fisher.
1928-1953	Beginning with Griffith's work, groundwork laid for molecular genetics.
1953	With the publication of Watson and Crick's model of DNA, molecular genetics begins explosive phase of development.

Although the chronology is highly simplified, the dates of 1866, 1900, 1925 (a mid-date), and 1930 could have been used to estimate the interval from 1866 to 1953. Each time span is multiplied by its respective coefficient and the sum of products is then divided by the number of time spans or coefficients used.

$$T = \frac{4.17\ (34) + 2.0\ (42) + 1.67\ (59) + 1.41\ (64) + 1.2\ (74)}{5}$$

$$= \frac{503}{5}$$

$$= 100.6$$

Thus the Watson-Crick breakthrough in genetics would have been predicted in 1930 to occur about 100 years from 1866, or in 1966. Because the Watson-Crick discovery actually occurred in 1953, the calculated time span exceeds the date of discovery by thirteen years. While this particular prediction is not too accurate, the method might have been used to approximate the date of discovery well before its actual occurrence. The generality of the predictive formula can be demonstrated by applying it to a discovery which occurred after a relatively compressed time interval—one of only nine years.

A discovery in isotope chemistry, which may be taken as another case of subsystem or sub-subsystem formation is well summarized by F. S. Soddy in the conclusion of his 1921 Nobel Award acceptance address.[25] His summary of the nine key events which led to his discovery in isotope chemistry is reproduced in the Appendix. After a methodological advance in 1905, several key findings (in 1807, 1909, 1911, *ca.* 1912, et al.) were brought together by Soddy's 1913 theoretical synthesis. By the same method, the date of this discovery might have been predicted:

$$T = \frac{4.17 \ (2) + 2.0 \ (4) + 1.67 \ (6) + 1.41 \ (7) + 1.2 \ (8)}{5}$$

$$= \frac{8.34 + 8.0 + 10.0 + 9.85 + 9.6}{5}$$

$$= 9.16$$

Thus the discovery might have been predicted to occur nine years after 1905, or in 1914—a year after its actual occurrence. Again the formula provides a crude estimate of the duration of subsystem formation or of the discovery date. The formula is further applied in chapters 3 and 5 on more actual discovery chronologies.

Human Memory Limits and Subsystem Formation

The eight cases of subsystem formation reviewed in this chapter reveal at least two common features: (1) each case was based on a synthesis of prior contributions; (2) the number of key contributions which culminated in each synthesis was relatively small. The eight cases include a total of fifty-six contributions—an average of seven contributions per case. It may be recalled that human short-term memory is capable of processing approximately seven items at one time. The fact that in each case approximately seven contributions were synthesized into discoveries or subsystems serves to demonstrate the possible influence of short-term memory in acts of scientific synthesis or discovery.

Various observers have noted the cumulative and

synthetic aspects of growth in certain areas of inquiry. For example, in a study of the discovery of spectral analysis Kedrov concludes that inventors Kirchoff and Bunsen did not use original data. They established relationships among known empirical findings, and carried the ideas of their predecessors to their logical conclusion. Kedrov states that a theoretical discovery occurs when the accumulation of empirical data can no longer progress without these data being brought into theoretical focus.[26] Another study reveals that new inventions are essentially recombinations and syntheses of previous inventions.[27] Tullock argues that the great unifying theories of science consist essentially of classification systems. "It is undeniably true that new discoveries are based on old discoveries."[28] In their work on the genesis of science Schwartz and Bishop attempted to demonstrate "how the work of many scientists has slowly evolved into a pattern and later into a discipline."[29]

Given the cumulative nature of subsystem formation, why does each formation embody an apparently small number of contributions? Price notes that "it seems to take a quorum of about 10 papers to produce a new one. . . ."[30] If human capacity to recall and manipulate cognitive entities is limited, then it would follow that the direct result of individual information processing must be correspondingly limited to what is cognitively manageable. Einstein noted that creative thought involves a "combinatory play" with physical elements, but that "full consciousness is a limit case which can never be fully accomplished. This seems to me connected with the fact called narrowness of consciousness (Enge des Bewusstseins)."[31] With regard to mathematical problem-solving, Pierre Boutroux has stated:

Memory is necessary to retain the data of the problem if we do not use them all from the beginning. We should risk forgetting them if the image of the objects under consideration were not constantly present to our mind and did not offer all of them to us at each instant.[32]

In conclusion, evidence in this chapter suggests the following interpretation: because of limited human information processing capacity, syntheses become periodically necessary as the number of basic contributions in a given area pushes the upper limits of the short term memory capacity of individual scientists. Such periodic syntheses make previous findings easier to remember and thus help to provide the conceptual economy requisite to further inquiry. Insofar as such syntheses periodically exist, they can provide one basis for predicting the formation and transformation of small or large conceptual systems. The growth and transformation of larger systems are treated in succeeding chapters.

Summary

Analysis of eight cases of subsystem formation supports the interpretation that such formation tends to occur when: (1) an adequate number of accepted, basic findings are available for synthesis; (2) the accumulation of basic findings approaches the upper limits of human short-term memory capacity; and (3) organization of findings is essential to further enquiry.

The time interval required for the formation of a given subsystem appears to be predictable on the basis of: (1) a discernible trend of similar, basic events;

(2) a pattern of regularity in the occurrence of these events; and (3) when approximately seven basic events have taken place.

The formations of sub-subsystems, subsystems, and of disciplinary systems appear to be similar phenomena. A basic concept might achieve no more than a relatively minor functional status within a system. In any case, the process of concept formation appears to have been subject to human information processing limitations, particularly that of short-term memory.

3

Formation of Systems

In the previous chapter the formation of disciplinary subsystems or subdisciplines was analyzed. It was noted that distinctions between subsystems and systems can be tentative and somewhat arbitrary; a growing subsystem is potentially the basis for a system. This chapter extends the previous one by first reviewing the formation and growth patterns of traditional systems, particularly mathematics and physics. Second, it discusses the formation of interdisciplinary or integrative systems, particularly the communication and behavioral sciences. Third, it assesses the role of human memory limits as a factor in the formation, growth, and differentiation of disciplinary systems.

System Formation and Growth

Before examining the emergence of disciplinary systems, the historical peculiarity of independent, simultaneous discoveries might first be noted. Several examples, including two cases previously discussed, are summarized below.[1]

Logarithms	Napier	1614	Burgi	1620
Calculus	Newton	1666	Leibniz	1673
Oxygen	Priestly	1774	Scheel	1777
Atomic Theory	Higgins	1789	Dalton	1814

Non-Euclidean geometry	Lobachevsky	1829	Bolyai	1832
Energy conservation	Meyer	1842	Joule	1847
Algebra of logic	Boole	1847	DeMorgan	1847
Evolution	Darwin	1858	Wallace	1858
Periodic Classification	Mendeleef	1869	Meyer	1869
Stereo-isomerism	van't Hoff	1874	Le Bel	1874

The frequent phenomenon of simultaneous discovery indicates that more than one inquirer responds to the same problem at the same time. Kedrov explains that no important scientific discovery comes unexpectedly, but that such discoveries are the culmination of long preparation.

> First there is a gradual accumulation of the necessary prerequisites for a decisive step in the discovery of a new truth, and then, when the prerequisites are all present, the development of scientific thought itself necessarily advances right up to the point of discovery. The discovery frequently consists in the fact that postulates and thoughts previously advanced as individual hypotheses and isolated empirical observations and facts are synthesized, as it were, merging into a single and integral generalization reflecting the new truth in a relatively complete form, for the given level of development of science.[2]

Such coincidental discoveries might be motivated by what Edward Boring calls the *zeitgeist,* or "spirit of the time."[3] Or, in accordance with Goffman and Newill's theory that human susceptibility to ideas is analogous to susceptibility to diseases, certain groups of investigators or entire disciplines can be "infected" with aspects of the same problem at the same time.[4]

One might reasonably hypothesize, then, that different disciplinary subsystems or entire disciplines could have common origins in the same problem. The dimensions of the underlying problem might be more fully revealed by examining similar disciplinary subsystems or systems which emerged at approximately the same time. In accordance with the analogy of the blind men studying the elephant, different scholars could discover different aspects of the same massive elephant.

Mathematics

The previous chapter reviewed the formation of geometry and the calculus as mathematical subsystems. This section summarizes the formation and growth of modern mathematics. According to Bell:

> Modern mathematics originated in five major advances of the seventeenth century: the analytic geometry of Fermat (1629) and Descartes (1637); the differential and integral calculus of Newton (1666, 1684) and Leibniz (1673, 1675); the combinatorial analysis (1654), particularly the mathematical theory of probability, of Fermat and Pascal; the higher arithmetic (c. 1630-65) of Fermat; the dynamics of Galileo (1591, 1612) and Newton (1661, 1684), and the universal gravitation (1666, 1684-87) of Newton.
>
> With these five, two further departures in new directions may be cited for their influence on subsequent advances: the synthetic projective geometry (1636-39) of Desargues and Pascal; the beginning of symbolic logic (1665-90) by Leibniz.[5]

Bell's summary reveals that all seven advances

occurred within a relatively compressed time interval. If Descartes' geometry (1637) and Newton's calculus (1666) are used as earliest and latest discovery dates, the interval is reduceable to 29 years. For this era, when communications were slow, these events are remarkably close together. The probability of a random event occurring within a given 50-year interval of, say, a 1,000 year span is 5 percent. According to the Multiplicative Law of Probability, the joint probability of seven independent events occurring in the same 50-year interval of 1,000 years is only 0.05 to the seventh power, the product of the separate probabilities.[6] It is not likely that the above mathematical advances were truly independent of one another. One might argue that different investigators "discovered" modern mathematics, or different aspects of the same system, at approximately the same time. The relatively simultaneous emergence of a group of mathematical subsystems apparently marked the formation of the modern mathematical disciplinary system.

Following its formative period, modern mathematics underwent a period of vigorous growth. Through the eighteenth century the calculus and its applications displaced geometry and astronomy from their twenty-century dominance of mathematical tradition.[7]

Struik summarizes trends in the nineteenth century as: (1) a liberation of mathematics from the demands of economic life and warfare; (2) the development of specialists interested in science for its own sake; and (3) specialization in "pure" or "applied" mathematics.

Mathematicians began to work in specialized fields; while Leibniz, Euler, and D'Alembert can

be described as "mathematicians" . . . we think of
Cauchy as an analyst, of Cayley as an algebraist,
of Steiner as a geometer (even a pure geometer)
and of Cantor as a pioneer in point set theory.
. . . The time was ripe for "mathematical physicists" followed by men learned in "mathematical
statistics" or "mathematical logic." Specialization
was broken only on the highest level of genius.[8]

By 1870 mathematics had become "an enormous and
unwieldy structure divided into a large number of
fields in which only specialists knew the way."[9]

A possibly valid but simplified analogy of
mathematical development is the growth pattern of a
tree.[10] The calculus might be viewed as a trunk formation which sprang essentially from analytic geometry,
plane geometry, algebra, trigonometry, and irrational
numbers. After a growth period of approximately 113
years (1687 to ca. 1800) several specialized branching
systems emerged from the trunk. A few branches were
initially similar to their numeric, algebraic or geometric
roots, but most of them represented the results of complex internal transformations during the growth
process. As the specialized branches exceeded their
optimum sizes and subdivided, new specialized
offshoots and new combinations developed. For example, projective, non-Euclidean, and differential
geometries developed essentially from Euclidean
geometry. The theory of games, on the other hand,
largely developed as a synthesis of integral and differential equations and topology. Such branching and
cross branching processes are, however, extremely
complex. Price points out the "virtual absence of any

general historical sense of the way science has been working for the last hundred years."[11]

The following three general breakdowns of mathematics, for different centuries, provide an image of subsystem and system change and reflect the fact that the number of basic categories tends to be restricted to a cognitively manageable number.[12]

	ca. 1700	1888	1964
1.	Plane geometry	Elliptic functions	Functions of real variable
2.	Algebra	Theory of numbers	Numbers and sets
3.	Trigonometry	Higher algebra	Algebra and Topology
4.	Higher arithmetic	Modern geometry	Geometry
5.	Calculus	Analytic geometry	Functions of complex variable
6.	Dynamics	Analysis	Functional and general analysis
7.	Combinatorial analysis	Astronomy	Probability theory
8.		Mathematical Physics	Differential and partial equations
9.			Cybernetics

Again, such changes are very complex and the impact of human memory limits on the transformation of the mathematical system is but one of several variables to consider. Other variables which also might influence evolution of mathematical concepts, such as cultural need, inadequacies of old concepts, utility and fruitfulness of new concepts, or symbolism, are summarized by Wilder.[13]

Two types of subsystems may now be distinguished—formative subsystems and branch specialization subsystems. Formative subsystems may be viewed as those which *converge* to form a disciplinary system and are thus analogous to *roots* of a tree. Branch subsystems are those which *diverge* from a maturing system, and are thus analogous to *branches* of a tree. Euclidian and non-Euclidian geometry, respectively, are examples of formative and branch subsystems. The branches of a mature system could be instrumental in forming a new system. Bell divides the long-run growth of mathematics into seven periods, in each of which there was a rise to maturity and a subsequent decline and fragmentary branching. Through each period, however, the stock of accumulated mathematical knowledge has continued to grow, and many contributions once associated with the names of particular men become anonymous.[14] In summary, if the tree analogy is not overdrawn, it could clarify the growth of various other disciplines. The circumscribed limits of human memory would then be analogous to the circumference of a formative or branch disciplinary subsystem.

Physics

In the previous chapter, the emergence of Newtonian mechanics was reviewed as a case of subsystem formation. Other subsystems in classical physics were forming along with Newtonian mechanics. The emergence of these other subsystems and the increasing autonomy of physical inquiry were a part of the process by which unified natural philosophy fragmented.[15] Von Laue and others note that several early key contributions in classical physics were made early in the seventeenth century. In 1600 Gilbert reported his observations on magnetism and coined the word electricity. Galileo made the first measurement of heat shortly after 1600 and in 1638 reported successful experiments in acoustics and mechanics. Snell stated his light refraction laws in 1621 and successful experiments in optics were announced later by Newton, Huygens and Grimaldi.[16]

The time interval in which these events occurred, approximately thirty-eight years, is again remarkably compressed. It might be said that natural philosophers "discovered" physics at approximately the same time, or that a disciplinary system became operative during this time. Following its birth, physics underwent a period of growth, was raised to "a new plateau of perfection and remained essentially stable and was elaborated only inwardly for more than a century."[17]

In the early nineteenth century, physics became increasingly specialized. Electricity had attained the rank of a science with the 1786 announcement of Coulomb's law. Later work by Ampère, Ohm, Faraday, and others was synthesized by Maxwell's decisive 1862 paper on electromagnetic radiation. Light interference and polarization were discovered in 1801 and 1809, and Maxwell related light to electricity and magnetism in his 1862 paper. Laplace synthesized mechanics in 1800 and further specialization led to such laws as Hamilton's "principle of least action" in 1886. Heat and thermodynamics developed rapidly from approximately 1800 to 1850. Chladni's 1802 work in acoustics was climaxed by the 1862 work of Helmholtz.[18]

Modern physics, largely an extension of the work of the above pioneers, began its development with the discoveries of such men as Planck, Einstein, Schrodinger, Heisenberg, Dirac, Pauli, de Broglie, and others. A contemporary work which covers "the internal structure of the whole system of theoretical physics," includes the following nine subdivisions: point mechanics, mechanics of systems, heat transfer, thermodynamics, kinetic theory, statistical mechanics, electricity and magnetism, optics, and the wave theory of matter.[19] A more elementary treatment embraces seven fields: mechanics, heat, sound, electricity, light, quanta, and nuclear physics.[20]

To summarize, classical physics passed through three phases: (1) a formative period extending approximately from Copernicus to Galileo (1543-1638); (2) a growth period from approximately 1638 to 1800; and (3) a maturing and differentiating period from approximately 1800 to 1870, which paved the way for the formation of new subsystems such as relativity and nuclear physics.

Similar formative, growth, and differentiation stages can be discerned in other traditional scientific disciplines, and estimates of their duration can be made. For example, the formative period of chemistry might be said to extend from Boyle (ca. 1661), the "father of chemistry," to the 1789 work of Lavoisier, which established chemistry on a scientific basis. The growth period extends from approximately 1789 to 1869, when Mendeleef and Meyer formulated their periodic laws and when general chemical journals were first published. By 1925 the specialized branches of atomic, physical, analytical, inorganic, and organic chemistry and biochemistry were all distinctly developed.[21] In biology, the work of such figures as Vesalius (1543), Harvey (1628), and Redi (1668) marks the start of a long formative era which extended at least to Linnaeus (1735). Biological inquiry attracted increasingly greater numbers of scientists and by the beginning of the nineteenth century specialization was well underway. By 1858, when Darwin and Wallace published their work on evolution, approximately five major branches of biology were well established: taxonomy, comparative anatomy, paleontology, embryology, and physiology.[22]

The formative period of geology ranges approximately from Steno, the "first modern geologist" (1669), to Hutton's theoretical synthesis (1785). The growth period extends from approximately 1785 to 1833, when Lyell published a comprehensive treatise. Specializations became increasingly narrow and by the end of the nineteenth century a general feeling existed among scientists that most specialized problems had been solved.[23] According to Bruner and Allport, the formative period in American scientific psychology extended from approximately 1870, when interest in experimentation became apparent, to 1888. The period from 1888 to approximately 1908 "gives the general impression of healthy growth"; in 1908, however, theoretical divisions were noticed and by 1928 specialization was the rule.[24]

Thus, development of the various disciplinary systems above, taken as examples, involved periods of formation, unified growth and differentiation or branching. The next section reviews the emergence of a more modern generation of disciplines—which is here, somewhat arbitrarily, called the integrative disciplines.

Integrative Systems

An interdisciplinary integrative movement of significant proportions appears to have gained considerable momentum within the last few years. This move-

ment is marked particularly by the relatively simultaneous emergence of the communication and behavioral
sciences, both of which have spread through preestab-
lished groups of disciplines—the humanities, physical
sciences, biological and social sciences. Thus the term
"integrative systems" or disciplines generally is applied
to the behavioral and communication-oriented disciplines. The concept of integrative disciplines may now
be elaborated, first by a discussion of communication
science and then by a discussion of the behavioral sciences.

As early as 1957 Colin Cherry depicted communication science as a broad scale movement seeking
integration and unity of diverse, specialized disciplines.
Though "by no means a unified study," communication science was based chiefly on work in languages
and coding, information theory, cybernetics, and the
methodology of inquiry.[25] By 1967 communication science had come to be viewed as not only interdisciplinary, but "supradisciplinary." Communication science
extended

> indeterminately across many fields of study in the
> life and behavioral sciences and the applied arts.
> . . . it lies along the often great cultural bound-
> aries which divide one way of seeing the world
> from another. . . .
> informational or communication theoretical
> methodology is destined to aid many disciplines
> and help their cross-fertilization and so engender
> new syntheses.[26]

Thus by 1967 the role of communication science
appeared to be clearer. The following 1957 and 1967

outlines of communication science reflect the changing
scope of the field over ten years.[27]

1957	1967

1. Signs, Language Communication	1. Signals
	   a. Sending
	   b. Receiving

2. Signal Analysis	2. Transmission
3. Statistical Theory of Communication	a. Physical
4. Logic of Communication	b. Sociopsychological
a. Syntactics	3. Situations
b. Semantics	a. Comparative
c. Pragmatics	b. Cross-cultural
5. Cognition and Recognition	4. Epistemology
	5. Axiology and Choice
	6. Rhetoric and Problem-solving

The behavioral sciences were conceived in the
1930s and emerged shortly after World War II as a
result of joint efforts by the Ford Foundation and
groups of scholars to deal synoptically with behavioral
problems. In 1956 the founding editors of the journal
Behavioral Science provided the following functional
description of the field:

If the fragments of multiple sciences were
brought together in a unitary behavioral science
. . . the uniformities among disciplines could be
recognized; better communication among them
established; generality of findings magnified;
additional benefits derived from comparing
theories in diverse fields, explaining both
similarities and differences; and the validity and
applicability of empirical work increased by

planning individual studies as components of an explicit mosaic of research strategy.[28]

In 1963 and 1964 the Behavioral Research Council made a distinction between the "older fields" of behavioral inquiry (anthropology, sociology, history, economics, political science, psychology, education) and the "newer fields." The newer fields include those of communication theory (information theory, cybernetics, linguistics, sign-behavior) and those involving preferential behavior (game theory, decision-making theory, value inquiry and general systems theory). Thus there appears to be a considerable overlap between the communication and behavioral sciences. Further general features of the newer behavioral sciences are summarized in Table 2.[29]

As of 1964 the behavioral sciences appeared to be in a state of growth and internal confusion.

The lines of demarcation between fields are unstable and confused. Some regard general systems theory as encompassing other areas. . . . Game theory is sometimes regarded as part of decision-making theory, which in turn is sometimes regarded as part of value inquiry. Some inquirers of sign behavior include linguistics as a subsection of sign behavior, while some linguistics hope to expand their area to include . . . communication theory.[30]

Nevertheless, behavioral science had swept through anthropology, zoology, statistics, sociology, psychology, psychiatry, political science, physiology, pharmacology,

TABLE 2
THE BEHAVIORAL SCIENCES

Field	Locus of Inquiry	Chief Founders
Information Theory	Effective coding, transmission and reception of messages in communication systems, without regard to value or significance of information involved in the communication process	Shannon and Weaver, 1948
Cybernetics	Regulative processes of physical, biological, and behavioral systems with special emphasis on feedback in machines and nervous systems.	Wiener, 1948
Linguistics	Language structures, principles underlying the organization of languages, historical changes and relations between languages or linguistic codes.	Bloomfield 1914, 1933
Sign Behavior	Verbal and non-verbal naming, signaling and symbolizing. Critical analysis and clarification of language and cognitive behavior.	Korzybski 1933 Morris 1938
Game Theory	Cooperative and competitive behavior patterns involving alternative choices and outcomes.	Von Neumann and Morgenstern 1944
Decision Theory	Aspects of human behavior in which choices are made among alternatives. Descriptive and normative study of decision-making.	Wald 1939
Value Inquiry	Behavior indicating preferences among alternative choices available to individuals and groups; the set of preferences that influence selections.	Perry 1926 Reid 1938
General Systems Theory	Models, principles and laws applying to generalized physical, biological or behavioral systems, or their subclases.	Lotka, 1925 Von Bertalanffy 1950

neurology, mathematics, linguistics, history, geography, genetics, economics, ecology, and biochemistry.[31]

The continuing program of *The American Behavioral Scientist* includes the following objectives:

> To help develop the sciences of information, classification, coding, storage, retrieval, supply and recycling of communication.
>
> To humanize the social sciences and introduce science into the humanities.
>
> To help the world intelligentsia achieve its community, its mission, and an acceptable level of influence over public policy.[32]

It is interesting to note that communication science and behavioral science share several common features and objectives: (1) both fields emerged almost simultaneously in the decade following World War II; (2) both have developed as large-scale movements rather than as single disciplines; (3) both seek integration of the sciences and the humanities, or intergroup disciplinary syntheses rather than more modest interdisciplinary syntheses; and (4) both fields claim information theory, cybernetics, semantics, general systems theory, and other areas.

Such similarities between behavioral science and communication science suggest the possibility of their origin in a common problem or of their gradual convergence as a response to a common need. Further, the relationship between communication, information and behavior does appear to be a close one, as Wiener emphasizes:

When I communicate with another person I impart a message to him . . . he returns a related message which contains information primarily accessible to him and not to me. When I control the actions of another person I communicate a message to him. . . .[33]

Hence communication, information, and behavior appear as counterparts of the same process; the occurrence of one required occurrence of the other two. Similarities of the communication and behavioral sciences are discussed further in chapter 4.

The formative patterns of individual behavioral or communication disciplines appear to be similar to those of the traditional disciplines reviewed in the previous chapter. An enterprising human mind synthesizes a small number of preexisting ideas. For example, Norbert Wiener states:

The whole background of my ideas on cybernetics lies in the record of my earlier work. Because I was interested in the theory of communication, I was forced to consider the theory of information and, above all, that partial information which our knowledge of one part of a system gives to us of the rest of it. Because I had studied harmonic analysis and had been aware that the problem of continuous spectre drives us back on the consideration of functions and curves too irregular to belong to the classical repertory of analysis, I formed a new respect for the irregular and a new concept of the essential irregularity of the universe. Because I had worked in the closest possible way with physicists and engineers, I knew that our data can never be precise. Because I had some contact with the complicated mechanism of the nervous system, I knew that the world about us is accessible only through a nervous system, and that our information concerning it is confined to what limited information the nervous system can transmit.[34]

In formulating their mathematical theory of communication, Shannon and Weaver acknowledged their fundamental dependence on the work of several predecessors: Nyquist (1924) and Hartley (1928), for early mathematical work; Hopf and others (1934), for generalization of the ergodic theorem; Folman's statistical mechanics (1938); Chandrasekhar's work in stochastic theory (1943); and Wiener's collaborative work (1948).[35] An early prediction of Shannon and Weaver's 1948 breakthrough could have been made by using three coefficients in the formula developed in the previous chapter:

$$T = \frac{4.16\,(4) + 2\,(10) + 1.67\,(14)}{3}$$

$$= 20 \text{ years.}$$

The breakthrough would have been predicted to occur twenty years from 1924 or in 1944, four years short of its actual occurrence. It might also be noted, for purposes of comparison, that the formative period in this instance is twenty-four years. The mathematical theory of communication, undergoing a unified growth period, gained in popularity and by 1960 some degree of specialization within the field was evident, as reflected by the six areas under discussion at the

Fourth London Symposium on Information Theory:
coding, detection, and statistical theory; telecommuni-
cation systems; human reaction to information; sensory information and biological models; learning
mechanisms; and classifications theory, syntactics and
semantics.[36] Thus after a formative period of twenty-
four years and a growth period of approximately
twelve years, the beginnings of specialized inquiry were
evident.

A similar formative and growth pattern is apparent in general systems theory. The formative period,
according to von Bertalanffy, extends from Lotka's
1925 work in mathematical biology to approximately
1950. In 1954, Young surveyed general systems theory
through a content analysis of the literature of several
natural and social sciences and professions.[37]. His survey revealed that general systems theory had, with considerable impact, penetrated these several fields. He
proposed four systematic categories within general systems theory and suggested a few potentially emergent
categories.

The significance of the behavioral and communication sciences will be further discussed in the chapters
which follow. It is now perhaps appropriate to summarize and compare the formative, growth, and differentiation periods of the disciplinary systems
reviewed so far. Table 3 indicates, for each discipline,
the years in each period and the corresponding percentages of the total time period.

The data in Table 3 are based on crude estimates
and provide no more than an approximate idea of the
proportionate time required for disciplinary formation, growth, and differentiation.

TABLE 3

FORMATIVE, GROWTH, AND DIFFERENTIATION
PERIODS OF SEVERAL DISCIPLINES

	Formation		Growth		Differen-tiation		Total
	Years	Percent	Years	Percent	Years	Percent	Years
Mathematics	125	40	113	37	70	23	308
Physics	95	29	162	50	70	21	327
Chemistry	128	48	80	30	56	22	264
Biology	122	50	65	27	58	23	245
Geology	116	50	48	21	67	29	231
Psychology	18	32	20	34	20	34	58
Information Theory	24		12		Unknown		
General Systems Theory	25		14		Unknown		

Although each period varies considerably, their average percentages of the total time (where available) may be calculated. The average formative period required 41 percent, the growth period 33 percent, and the differentiation period 26 percent of the total time span. Hence, if continued growth and specialization occur in information theory and general systems theory, these disciplinary systems could be reasonably well differentiated by the year 1978. But the assumptions underlying such an estimate are, of course, tenuous. Information theory or general systems theory might not follow the same growth pattern as the more traditional disciplines.

Human Memory Span and Systems

In the days of Aristotle knowledge was meager, relative to present standards. It was comparatively easy to summarize the few recorded observations and build generalizations to cover them. But humans possess a "time-binding" capacity which supports the accumulation of knowledge.

> to become acquainted with an object, we must not only explore it from all possible points of view and put it in contact with as many nerve centers as we can, as this is an essential condition of knowing . . . our nerve centers must summarize the partial, abstracted, specific pictures . . . we have a capacity to collect all known experiences of different individuals. Such a capacity increases enormously the number of observations a single individual can handle, and so our acquaintance with the world . . . becomes more refined and exact.[38]

The sustained accumulation and refinement of experience resulted in a stock of knowledge which probably would have exceeded the cognitive grasp of most literate individuals very early in history, had they been exposed to it. With the occurrence of such Renaissance events as the secularization of inquiry, scientific empiricism, rediscovery and scrutiny of classical texts, invention of the printing press and discovery of the New World, a flood of recorded experiences became available to scholars. One historian goes so far as to say, "Henceforth, no single scholar would ever again dare to tackle all branches of human knowledge, and the best of them restricted their investigations to given fields."[39] While such later figures as Leibniz might have been exceptions, for they did dare to tackle the sum of human knowledge, inquiry became increasingly specialized as the polygraphers gave way to monographers and several rudimentary scientific disciplines were formed.[40]

In the seventeenth century one could still find single individuals who had mastered all three fields of physics, chemistry, and astronomy.[41] In Kant's day a general grasp of all knowledge was still thought to be possible, but the title of metaphysician lacked prestige.[42]

At the beginning of the nineteenth century, three trends were apparent, according to Price: (1) the cessation of "catch-all" scientific societies and the proliferation of societies limited to one area; (2) the rise of specialized journals designed to cover autonomous disciplines; and (3) the rise of scientific abstracts to increase the assimilatory effectiveness of specialists.[43]

By the twentieth century, individuals who claimed mastery of their own disciplines were rare. Finally, Einstein offered the "outrageous view" that the unity of individual experience must be sacrificed to obtain unity of scientific experience. The universe was no longer thought to be "a reflection in the human mind; on the contrary, the human mind has limits which are in urgent need of definition."[44] Thus Einstein acknowledged the inadequacy of the individual cognitive span, relative to accumulated experience. Present trends in science appear to point out further the weakness of the intellectual foot soldier. For example, Price points out the use of big teams in science and predicts their continued existence along with the increased production of multi-authored papers; if this trend continues, "by 1980 the single author paper will be extinct."[45]

A peculiar feature of many disciplinary systems is

the relatively restricted number of subdisciplines or subsystems of which they are comprised. A hierarchical classification of the major contemporary sciences, for example, shows that the sciences consist of five to eight subfields.[46] Like the subdisciplines and individual discoveries considered in the previous chapter, each contemporary science appears to be presented in such a way that it is a cognitively manageable system of entities.

The hierarchical spans of contemporary sciences could be extended in depth as well as in breadth. However, an overextension of such spans, either horizontally or vertically, would make them too long and unmanageable from a human information processing standpoint.

Such classificatory spans are similar to the span of control used in pyramidal human organizations. Ideally, each superior supervises the efforts of an optimum or manageable number of subordinates.

There have been many attempts to specify exactly how many persons one man can effectively supervise—the number stated by various writers ranging from three to around fifteen. . . . The maximum size of an effective unit is limited basically by the ability of that unit to solve its problems of internal communication.

The pyramidal form typical of organizations is therefore a consequence of: (1) the need for coordination of individual activities, (2) the effectiveness of the individual nervous system as a coordinating mechanism, and (3) the limits upon the effective span of this mechanism.[47]

In addition to an optimum span of control, at each level in the pyramidal organization, an optimum number of levels is required in order that the organization function as a viable operational entity with adequate internal communications. Thus, within administrative science the "span of control" principle is augmented by its complementary principle of optimum organizational levels. One principle states that organizations should be compressed horizontally and the other that organizations should be compressed vertically.[48] Such principles might well apply to organizations of human knowledge. At any rate, the main hypothesis of this inquiry is that humans have in fact tended to restrict their organizations of knowledge to cognitively manageable configurations.

Disciplinary systems are stratified in other ways, but the number of stratifications tends to be restricted. For example, Figure 2 displays a breakdown of psychology, philosophy and history by various systems or schools of interpretation. In addition, disciplinary cognitive styles are listed.[49]

The existence of various systems and schools of interpretation suggests that scholars might often have preferred or required cognitively convenient and harmonious outlooks over simultaneously broader and deeper outlooks. Heidbreder states:

> System after system announces its principles, each imposes its order on the facts that arrest its attention, and each puts its case with a degree of plausibility. The difficulty is that they all do so and that they are all more or less at odds with each other. . . . The more definitely a system

draws the lines of its pattern, the more rigidly it selects its facts; the clearest and most consistent systems are those most given to denials and exclusions.[50]

Psychological Systems	*Philosophical Systems*
1. Structuralism	1. Naturalism
2. Pragmatism	2. Pragmatism
3. Functionalism	3. Dualism
4. Behaviorism	4. Realism
5. Dynamicism	5. Intuitionism
6. Gestaltism	6. Mysticism
7. Psychoanalysis	7. Idealism

Historical Schools	*Disciplinary Cognitive Styles*
1. Biographical	1. Literary
2. Idealism	2. Academic
3. Technological	3. Eristic
4. Economic	4. Symbolic
5. Geographical	5. Postulational
6. Sociological	6. Formal
7. Eclectic	

Figure 2.—Disciplinary Schools and Cognitive Styles

Moreover, the restricted number of schools or systems in each realm of inquiry suggests that human ways of looking at systems are correspondingly restricted to what is cognitively manageable.

Summary

The formative patterns of disciplinary systems resemble those of the subsystems reviewed in the previous chapter. The nearly simultaneous emergence of a set of similar subsystems apparently culminates in the formation of a disciplinary system. This phenomenon is analogous to the historically frequent incidence of independent, simultaneous discovery by two or more men. The cases studied suggest that disciplines, as well as concepts, can be "discovered" by several individuals at the same time. A subsystem or subdiscipline concept can provide the basis for organization of an entire disciplinary system if it proves to possess sufficient unifying power.

In each case of disciplinary development, the relatively distinct periods of formation, growth and differentiation could be discerned. The transformation of disciplinary subsystems and systems appears to be influenced by the human tendency to restrict increasingly larger bodies of knowledge to cognitively manageable proportions. The typical human response to an excess of accumulated knowledge is specialization of inquiry or application.

The growth and spread of the communication and behavioral sciences suggests the occurrence of a large-scale integrative movement—one which could potentially unify the sum of accumulated human knowledge. The communication and behavioral sciences emerged concurrently around 1950, possibly as simultaneous responses to a common problem. Both fields are supradisciplinary and they share many aims. Collectively, these disciplines seek optimal communication among men, machines and nature. They focus on systematic intrapersonal and interpersonal communication in order to promote adaptive behavior in the cooperative or competitive pursuit of valued ends. Their formative and growth patterns appear to be similar to those of traditional disciplines. The behavioral and communication sciences have not yet grown to the point where marked specialization, in the traditional sense, is necessary. The precise nature and extent of specialization in these sciences remains to be seen.

Thus with both the continuous accumulation of recorded experience and a relatively fixed and limited human information processing capability, specialization of inquiry has become progressively necessary. Disciplinary systems, as products of human cognition, reflect the attributes and limitations of human cognition. Disciplines tend to consist of approximately seven subdisciplines; this fact indicates the imposition of man's short term memory limitations on his organizations of knowledge. Disciplines appear to be organized largely for cognitive manageability, and are thus probably seriously restricted in scope and depth.

4

Toward a Suprasystem

So far, the formation and transformation of disciplinary subsystems and systems have been discussed, particularly from the standpoint of how human memory limits might intervene in such processes. This chapter extends the discussion to larger, more comprehensive systems of knowledge and attempts to demonstrate how human memory limits are continuously operative in shaping such comprehensive systems.

Prototype Suprasystems

As defined earlier, a suprasystem consists of a comprehensive, working system of man's knowledge. The following historical examples of general theoretical classifications reflect various conceptions of such comprehensive systems.[1]

Plato: Useful arts, music, gymnastics, mathematics, dialectics.

Aristotle: Economics, politics, law, productive art, mathematics, physics, theology.

Varro: Grammar, dialectics, rhetoric, geometry, arithmetic, astrology, music, medicine, architecture.

Capella: Arithmetic, music, geometry, astronomy, grammar, rhetoric, dialectics (the seven liberal arts).

Coleridge: Pure sciences—seven divisions
                Mixed sciences—five divisions
                Applied sciences—five divisions

Compte: Mathematics, astronomy, physics, chemistry, physiology, social physics.

Spencer: Logic, mathematics, mechanics, physics, astronomy, geology, psychology, sociology.

Of forty classification systems summarized by Richardson, including those above, the number of major subdivisions per classification system ranges between three and eleven. The mean, median, and mode number of subdivisions per classification system is, respectively, 6.07, 6.30 and 7.00. Two-thirds of all the classifications systems, whether ancient or modern, have between five and nine major subdivisions.[2] In short, such general theoretical systems tend to consist of approximately seven major categories.

The "seven liberal arts," listed above after Capella, has evoked considerable historical interest because of its survival and dominance. For over a thousand years it was the chief scholastic system of knowledge. It consisted of four branches in the mathematical quadrivium—arithmetic (numbers at rest), music (numbers in motion), geometry (magnitudes at rest), and astronomy (magnitudes in motion).[3] The quadrivium, probably due to Archytas (ca. 400 B.C.), was united with the trivium of grammar, rhetoric and dialectics around 440 A.D. This union of the quadrivium and trivium apparently highlighted the complementary

nature of the seven components, meeting Plato's classificatory requirements of "natural relationship" and
"intercommunication."[4] The complementary and
interdependent nature of the seven components was
emphasized by such scholars as Cicero and Hugh of
St. Victor.[5] Colin Cherry further states that the requisite of a functional organization is that its members or
elements be "in communication" with each other; a
condition of communication is the sharing of
behavior.[6] The hypothetical position of this inquiry is
that an average of seven elements is a cognitively
optimum number for such intercommunication and
reciprocity.

Various classification theorists, including Sayers,
Bliss, Dewey, and Ranganathan, have stated the necessity of building mnemonic features into classification
schemes.[7] In particular, Ranganathan states that a
given "System of Knowledge" is a result of the group-
ing and abstraction process forced by man's mental
and neurological limitations.

> The potency of forming many groups would have
> been increasingly realized . . . with the evolution
> of the cortex of the brain. . . . this inherent ten-
> dency to rank . . . is a result of the finiteness of
> speed of the nervous impulse within the human
> body. Finite speed gives rise to rank, sequence
> and structure.[8]

The finite speed of the nervous impulse is apparently a basic feature of the use of short term memory
when immediate and simultaneous access to all elements of a problem is required. Descartes found it

necessary to automatize recall to reduce the demands made on short term memory; essential elements of the problem had to be simultaneously available.

> I would run them over from time to time, keeping the imagination moving continuously in such a way that while it is intuitively perceiving each fact it simultaneously passes on to the next; and this I would do until I had learned to pass from the first to the last so quickly that no stage in the process was left to the care of memory, but I seemed to have the whole in intuition before me at the same time.[9]

It appears that the task of building comprehensive classification systems is as subject to short-term memory limits as any other difficult task.

Contemporary Sub-suprasystems

The contemporary circle of knowledge, other than applied or technical knowledge, is frequently described in terms of four categories: (1) humanities, 2) physical sciences, (3) biological sciences, (4) social sciences.[10] In this study, these four broad areas are treated as sub-suprasystems, each of which is commonly presented as a set consisting of approximately seven disciplinary systems.[11]

The emergence of the following four sub-supra-systems—the humanities and the physical, biological, and social sciences—may be viewed as successive, overlapping movements.

| | Physical | Biological | Social |
Humanities	Sciences	Sciences	Sciences
1 History	Astronomy	Taxonomy	History
2 Philosophy	Chemistry		
3 Religion	Geology		
4 Literature	Mineralogy	Physiology	Economics
5 Arts			
6	Physics	Genetics	Anthropology
7		Evolution	Psychology
8		Ecology	

Hoselitz renders the following interpretation:

1. The intellectual climate of opinion during the Middle Ages and the period of the Renaissance was predominantly humanistic. . . . natural science, although not completely dormant, yet is noticeably alive only on the periphery.

2. With the beginning of the sixteenth century, natural science began to advance but . . . the major scientific interest of the age was still lodged in the humanities.

3. The latter half of the seventeenth century and the first half of the eighteenth century were periods in which the interest in natural science was supreme. . . . the great new event. . . . was the advance and victory of natural science as a way of looking at the world, which led to the overtaking and overshadowing of the historical point of view by the scientific point of view.

4. We find during the one hundred and fifty years beginning in the second decade of the seventeenth century an imposing array of

achievements . . . in the field of biological and physical sciences, while the social sciences remain almost completely stagnant.

5. The revival of interest in social science occurred in the middle of the eighteenth century.[12]

By the end of the nineteenth century the social sciences were established in Europe and America.

Parsons also notes that the modern form of intellectual disciplines originated during the Renaissance. However, he emphasizes a prolonged dominance of the humanities, which comprised the core of higher learning in the Western world and maintained a virtual monopoly among educated classes until the middle of the nineteenth century. Despite the great, early scientific achievements, the influence of the natural sciences did not rival that of the humanities until well into the nineteenth century.[13]

In order to demonstrate further the successive and overlapping emergence of these groups of disciplines, the rise and growth of the natural sciences is depicted by Price's exponential growth and saturation curve, which is reproduced in Figure 3[14] (on page 73).

Price explains the projected leveling off tendency in science as a matter of scientific maturity and resultant saturation.

It is essential to the nature of the case that science go through a period of vigorous growth and that there has now come a sort of post-adolescent hiatus, and the growth is done and science has its adult stature. . . . Science has become . . . a saturated activity of mankind, taking as high a proportion of our expenditure in brains and money as it can attain. We have not reached that stage quite yet, but it is only a very short time before we will—less than a human generation.[15]

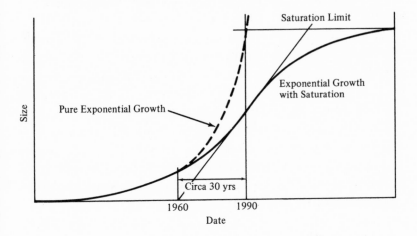

Figure 3.—Growth and Saturation of Science

In a similar fashion, the development of American social science has been described analogically in terms of formation, growth, and maturity. The "long formative period before 1860 may be characterized as one of emergence."[16] The growth and establishment of the social sciences represented a collective response to the increasing frequency and complexity of social problems occurring between 1750 and 1860. From 1860 to 1900 and later, the social sciences "underwent important transformations and enjoyed a remarkable period of growth."[17] After a period of rapid growth and differentiation, the excessive effects of specialization were somewhat ameliorated. "The border lines between the social disciplines began to disappear and overlappings became more numerous. The problem of jurisdiction, so absorbing in the nineties, has ceased to concern the investigator and student in any vital manner. . . ."[18]

In summary, the four sub-suprasystems emerged somewhat successively but with considerable overlapping. Their temporal boundaries are not sufficiently discrete for precise chronological analysis or prognosis. Generally, the humanities appear to have been displaced from their dominant position by the natural sciences. The natural sciences, however, show symptoms of forthcoming maturity and subsequent decline. The social sciences emerged more recently and their future status is uncertain. The next section discusses the emergence of what is regarded herein as a fifth sub-suprasystem—the integrative disciplines which were discussed in the last chapter.

Integrative Sub-suprasystem

Innumerable criticisms about the present system of man's knowledge have been registered in the last few decades. Generally, these criticisms mention: (1) the lack of unity and communication within one or a few related disciplines; or (2) the divergence and lack of communicative rapport between the sciences and humanities. The total problem is too complex for brief or singular treatment, but a few of its facets can be quickly considered.

Many critical and diagnostic attempts about the problems of man's knowledge have focused on one or a few disciplines. The unity of science movement, for example, sought to ameliorate the fragmentary condition of the sciences. One representative of the movement, John Dewey, viewed nationalistic, class, commer-

cial, racial, and religious interests as often contradis-
tinct from, and opposed to, the unity and use of science.[19] Similar critical attempts are carried on in social
sciences and humanities, but there appears to be a current recognition that the humanities or social sciences
cannot be adequately treated as isolates.[20] Vannevar
Bush has acknowledged that man's epistemological and
cognitive needs cannot be served by science alone.[21]

Other critical and diagnostic attempts are of much
wider scope, and encompass all major disciplinary
groups. For example, Matson urges a rapprochement
between the natural and social sciences and
humanities, in order that man may recapture the
unified view of the world that was fractured with the
adoption of Newtonian mechanics as a model of
interpretation of the world and a divorce of intellectual
from spiritual outlooks.[22] R. G. H. Siu argues for the
same natural, social, and humanistic integration, but
would add to it a synthetic Oriental-Occidental out-
look. He urges a reevaluation of the early compromise
between competitors in science and religion, achieved
through the gimmick of separating the spiritual from
the material realms. "With this convenient division of
fields of inquiry into two blocs, one was recognized as
the proper influential sphere of science and the other
of religion."[23] Jones likewise proposes a reconciliation
of the sciences and humanities to provide a general
conceptual scheme or unified world view.[24] These various commentaries suggest the need for more than a
mild form of interdisciplinarity which unites a few disciplines; they suggest the need for coordination in all
avenues of knowledge—the empirical, rational, practical, intuitive, and even the mystic.[25]

To the extent that relationships among the four

sub-suprasystems have been unclear, one might reasonably expect proportionate compensating responses to occur. Such responses appear to be under way as part of the integrative movement discussed in the previous chapter—the emergence of the behavioral and communication sciences. Whether the behavioral sciences and the communication sciences are of the same movement is a question for future historians to decide.

Certain trends, however, may be interpreted. First, as indicated in the previous chapter, the probability of several unrelated disciplines emerging at random within the same ten-or-twenty-year period within a 1,000-year period is extremely remote, perhaps less than 1 percent. The relatively simultaneous emergence of the integrative disciplines suggests their common origin in the same problem. Second, the integrative disciplines have penetrated all four sub-suprasystems. For example, concepts of information theory and cybernetics published in 1948 by Shannon and Wiener had by 1955 diffused through the fields of communications engineering, psychology, physiology, physics, linguistics, biology, sociology, optics, statistics, and journalism—in that order.[26] General systems theory emerged from and responded to a "secret trend" in various disciplines. In 1953 Boulding communicated to von Bertalanffy:

> I seem to have come to much the same conclusion as you have reached, though approaching it from the direction of economics and the social sciences rather than from biology. . . . I am sure that there are many people all over the world who have come essentially to the same position that we have,

but we are widely scattered and do not know each other, so difficult it is to cross the boundaries of the disciplines.[27]

The conceptual base of political science was drastically altered by the behavioral movement, particularly by cybernetics, general systems theory, and decision theory.[28] The simultaneous emergence of the behavioral and communication sciences, as well as their similarity of function and impact, suggests the possibility that they did have common problematic origins or at least a rapid convergence.

Other integrative efforts appear to be under way in areas besides the behavioral or communication sciences. For example, classification theorists have proposed new comprehensive integrative schemes but appear still to labor under the constraint of human short term memory limits. A member of the Classification Research Group has established the following scheme, based on a theory of integrative levels:

1. Fundamental
2. Sub-atomic
3. Atomic
4. Molecular
5. Cellular
6. Bio-morphic
7. Communal
8. National

Each level, in turn, is divided into eight active and eight passive categories.[29] The restricted number of levels and categories should, however, accord with requirements of human cognitive manageability.

A Soviet classification theorist urges the establishment of objectively based scientific classifications —those which accord with nature—rather than the entertainment of subjectively based schemes which are designed primarily to comport with human cognitive operations. However, he then proposes an "objectively" based evolutionary classification of knowledge consisting of approximately seven categories.[30] Here, too, transcendence of the human frame of reference by humans appears to be difficult if not impossible.

Toward a Suprasystem: World Encyclopedia Concept

The evolution and survival of large subsuprasystems raises the question of whether the formation of a suprasystem of knowledge is underway. If so, what form could such a suprasystem take? The existence of prototype suprasystems, discussed early in this chapter, affords some degree of historical precedence in support of the notion that a suprasystem could be developing. The prototype suprasystems have tended to consist of approximately seven major components. However, the contemporary circle of knowledge, as commonly represented, consists of only four major components with the possible emergence of a fifth integrative component. Thus, it is conceivable that the contemporary system of knowledge could lack approximately two major components in order to be fully functional as a cognitively viable system of knowledge. If these speculations are correct, it would appear that a suprasystem could be forming.

What form might such a suprasystem take? Several possibilities present themselves. First, to a considerable extent a suprasystem could be a codification of existing knowledge, encompassing present sub-suprasystems and any future ones as they emerge. Figure 4 illustrates the successive emergence of these sub-suprasystems. The chronological position of these sub-suprasystems is, however, only very approximate. Such long run movements do not lend themselves to precise or simplified temporal representation.

A second possible configuration for a suprasystem might parallel something like familiar conceptions of the unity of science. According to Caws, such familiar conceptions include: (1) unity as a reduction to a common basis; (2) unity as synthesis into total system; and (3) unity as the construction of an encyclopedia.[31] Thus, a suprasystem could require or result in the encyclopedic reduction, synthesis and systematization of knowledge.

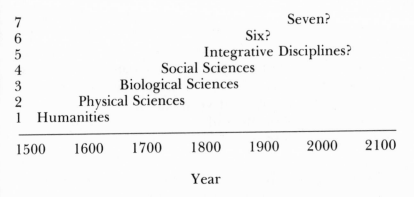

Figure 4.—Emergence of Sub-suprasystems

A third possible configuration of a suprasystem, accordingly, is that of a world encyclopedia or world brain.[32] A. C. Clarke, among others, has predicted the operation of a world brain by approximately 2100 A.D.[33] A world encyclopedia was proposed as early as

1936 by H. G. Wells as a result of his uneasiness over
the ignorance surrounding the tenuous settlement of
World War I. He argued that statesmen knew hardly
anything about the consequence of their acts; nor did
they even know what was to be known.

> Possibly all the knowledge . . . needed to establish
> a wise and stable settlement of the world's affairs
> in 1919 existed in bits and fragments . . . but prac-
> tically nothing had been done to draw that knowl-
> edge and these ideas together into a comprehen-
> sive conception of the world. . . .
> without a World Encyclopedia to hold men's
> minds together in something like a common
> interpretation of reality, there is no hope what-
> ever of anything but an accidental and transitory
> alleviation of any of our world troubles.[34]

Wells envisioned a world encyclopedia that would
reorganize the world's education and information,
through the dynamic growth, extension, revision and
replacement of its content; it would provide for the
testing of statements and verification of facts, serving
the role of a politically and economically disinterested,
"undogmatic Bible" to all of humanity. It would

> bring together into close juxtaposition and under
> critical scrutiny many apparently conflicting sys-
> tems of statement. It might act . . . as an organ
> of adjustment and adjudication, a clearing house
> of misunderstandings; it would be deliberately a
> synthesis and so act as a flux and a filter for a
> very great quantity of human misapprehension.

> . . . a World Encyclopedia must have a perennial life . . . with a progressive, adaptable and recuperative quality. . . .[35]

The problem posed by Wells has persisted, and several indirect variations of the World Encyclopedia have been proposed by different men in the last few years. For example, Boulding proposed in 1956 a new science of "eiconics," or theoretical imagery to serve as a basic form for the coherent unification of empirical data. Such images would consist of "minimum knowledge," not the maximum, serving as a "general theory of the empirical world; something which lies between the extreme generality of mathematics and the particularity of particular disciplines."[36] In 1959, Lasswell proposed a "Social Planetarium"—a series of research or seminar rooms equipped to present vivid simulations of past or future natural or cultural phenomena. Such presentations could assist research and social policy determination by making apparent various knowledge gaps.[37]

In 1960, Weiss demonstrated that bodies of knowledge tend to grow in a manner analogous to the growth of organisms; that is, through the assimilation rather than the accretion of nutrients.[38] Churchman proposed in 1961 the establishment of a "World Information Center," which would assess new research findings against accumulated findings in order to identify new findings as either redundant, not properly derived from the evidence, inconsistent with previous findings, or more supportive of certain theses and less supportive of others.[39] In 1965, de Grazia announced operation of the "World Reference System" for the social and behavioral sciences, and Watson Davis proposed the idea of a universal or world brain, much on the order of that proposed by Wells in 1937, but with an emphasis on utilization of computer technology.[40] Deutsch anticipates the large-scale use of theories and models as dynamic configurations for the evaluation, organization, and communication of knowledge.[41]

As time passes, the idea of a world encyclopedia seems to be less grandiose and utopian. It can be argued that the rudiments of a world encyclopedia exist today. According to von Bertalanffy, "a unitary conception of the world may be based . . . on the isomorphy of laws in different fields."[42] Boulding has defined general systems theory as "the skeleton of science in the sense that it aims to provide a framework or structure of systems on which to hang the flesh and blood of particular disciplines . . . in an orderly and coherent corpus of knowledge."[43] In biology, it has been demonstrated that different models, as subsystems of a general system, can be related in different ways for various types of problems. Such models may be applied individually or collectively to a problem in an alternative or simultaneous manner.[44] The systematic exploitation of models appears, then, as an alternative to a monolithic system of knowledge. Goffman and Newell observe:

> Since the process of transmitting ideas . . . is not a single process within a population but a collection of interacting processes within subpopulations, it would seem that the notion of an all-encompassing information retrieval system spanning the totality of knowledge should be replaced by the notion of small dynamic inter-

related systems that appear when needed and disappear when not needed.[45]

Various other forms of a potentially emergent
suprasystem are possible, and the topic has not been
exhaustively treated in this section. The suprasystem
has been viewed as potential codification of existing
and emergent sub-suprasystems, as a systematic
synthesis of reduced knowledge, and as a world encyclopedia. These three conceptions should be complementary rather than mutually contradictory.

From a cognitive standpoint, the formation of a
suprasystem appears to be not only desirable but
necessary. Heilprin observes that the creative union of
concepts takes place for only a short time—possible for
the brief duration of short-term memory.

> Our spans of attention and detail limit how much
> we can observe, and of how much we can be
> aware. Our mental processes in some way resem-
> ble those of a small bug crawling over an enor-
> mous canvas. At any given moment the bug (and
> we) perceive only a narrow horizon.[46]

A similar view on human cognition is used by
Reiser to justify the establishment of collective social
cognition in the form of a world brain.

> Our brains are prismatic—each facet of our
> reasoning machinery reflects a fragmentary part
> of the whole, which can only with great difficulty
> be resynthesized into a single master vision. Our
> thinking apparatus is a kind of cortical analyzer

. . . which breaks up the harmony of the cosmos into many separate chords.
If we fail to provide the machinery for such a world brain, all humanity will be headed for destruction.[47]

Summary

General theoretical classifications, treated herein as prototype suprasystems, have tended to consist of seven major categories. This fact reflects their mnemonic character. The contemporary circle of knowledge, however, is commonly described as an aggregate of only four sub-suprasystems: the humanities, physical sciences, biological sciences, and social sciences. Because cognitively viable general classification schemes have tended to consist of seven major subdivisions, the present circle of knowledge with its four subdivisions seems to be comparatively deficient. It not only lacks what might be a requisite number of components, but some critics have stated that these components do not interact appropriately. These four large components, or sub-suprasystems, do, however, each consist of approximately seven disciplinary systems and each one appears to be relatively complete on its own.

The contemporary sub-suprasystems emerged since the Renaissance apparently in serial order. The long dominance of the humanities was ended by the ascendance and dominance of the physical and biological sciences. These sciences now show signs of maturity. The rise of the social sciences is comparatively recent, and it is probably too early to judge just how mature the social sciences are.

Several recent critical and diagnostic attempts

have indicated a serious lack of rapport and communication within and among the humanities and the natural and social sciences. As a possible reaction to this lack of communication and rapport between the sciences and humanities an integrative movement of sub-suprasystem proportions, in the form of the communication and behavioral sciences, appears to have emerged during a relatively short period in the last few decades. This movement has penetrated and to some extent brought about a rapprochement between the sciences and humanities. Other recent integrative attempts, as for example those by classification theorists, continue to reflect the human cognitive constraints of short-term memory.

The apparent emergence and impact of an integrative or fifth sub-suprasystem renders some support to the contention that a suprasystem of human knowledge is emerging. The evolution of such a suprasystem could possibly involve: (1) a codification of existing and future sub-suprasystems; (2) the encyclopedic reduction, synthesis, and systematization of knowledge; and (3) the operation of a world encyclopedia or world brain. Nevertheless, human cognitive constraints appear to inhibit or prevent much more than a fragmentary vision of the universe, or for that matter of communicated experience.

5

Information Science as a Disciplinary System

This chapter reviews the emergence and subsequent development of information science within its wider disciplinary framework. Information science, that area of inquiry which focuses on information phenomena, processes and systems, is approached as one of a set of communication or behavioral disciplines which emerged simultaneously around the time of World War II. Consequently, an attempt is made to discern the evolution of relationships between information science and other disciplinary members of its set. First the internal development and growth of information science are reviewed. Second, possible relationships and roles of information science within a potentially emergent suprasystem of human knowledge are discussed. The reader will note that the disciplinary systems concepts developed in earlier chapters are used to interpret the formation and growth of information science.

Emergence of Information Science

The emergence of information science is probably too recent to permit its definitive historical reconstruction, or even more than its ephemeral definition. It might be tempting to equate the emergence of documentation, as is occasionally done, with that of information science. Documentation has been defined as "the process of collecting and subject classifying all the records of new observations and making them available, at need, to the discoverer or the inventor."[1] But a history of information science vis-à-vis documentation, only one of its important tributaries, would not qualify as complete history. It would appear that the history of information science is in part the history of all its contributory disciplines as well as an account of other factors involved in its emergence. The following discussion is not a comprehensive recapitulation of the complex emergence of information science but only a prelude to considering its future development. Documentation and information retrieval, to be discussed later, are viewed as archetypes of information science.

Mohrhardt provides the following landmark chronology of the development of documentation:[2]

1895   Institut International de Bibliographie (Belgium) (founded by Henri La Fontaine and Paul Otlet)
1909   Special Libraries Association (U.S.A.)
1924   Association of Special Libraries and Information Bureaux (England)
1926   Science Service (initiation of documentation activities, Watson Davis)
1931   Institut International de Documentation (redesignation of Institut International de Bibliographie)
1934   *Traité de Documentation* published by Paul Otlet
1934   Bibliofilm Service (established at U.S. Department of Agriculture Library)
1935   American Documentation Institute
1938   Federation Internationale de Documentation (redesignation of Institut International de Documentation)
1945   *Journal of Documentation*
        Vannevar Bush proposed fundamental innovations

1948   *Documentation* published by Bradford
        The Royal Society Scientific Information Conference
        (London)
1958   International Conference on Scientific Information
        (Washington, D.C.)

Although the chronology differs slightly from others presented in this study, it does reveal several key conceptual shifts and developments. The formative pattern of documentation appears to be similar to that of other disciplinary subsystems or systems, judging by the applicability of the formula developed in Chapter II:

$$T = \frac{4.17 \ (14) + 2.0 \ (29) + 1.67 \ (31) + 1.41 \ (36) + 1.2 \ (39)}{5}$$

= 53.5 years.

Thus a key synthesis might have been expected approximately 53 years after 1895, or in 1948. Publication by Vannevar Bush of a key article in 1945 and of Bradford's work in 1948 may be regarded as key syntheses, in addition to other events occurring during that period.[3]

Both Bush and Bradford offered definitive conceptualizations of the tasks of documentation. Although the scope of their treatments centered on physical aspects of documents and their use, they both introduced questions of far wider scope. Bush was particularly concerned with the augmentation of human intellect through access to artificial memory. His concepts thereby mark an expansion of the documentation paradigm and a transition to that of information storage and retrieval, which will be discussed shortly.

As reflected in the outlines of *Current Research and*

Development in Scientific Documentation, the major categories of documentation in 1957 were (1) organization of information, (2) equipment for storage and retrieval, (3) mechanical translation, and various emergent concerns such as the information needs of scientists and potential contributions of other fields to documentation. By 1959 the information needs of scientists became a fourth chief topic, and interest in problem-solving was emerging. By 1966 documentation had expanded to include nine topics.[4]

1. Information need and uses
2. Documentation creation and copying
3. Language analysis
4. Translation
5. Abstracting and Classification
6. System Design
7. Analysis and Evaluation of Systems
8. Pattern Recognition
9. Adaptive systems; artificial intelligence

The expansion of documentation evoked new questions concerning its proper locus and scope, with attendant terminological confusion. In 1964 Mohrhardt defined documentation as an integrative discipline of the communication sciences, but noted that "basically, we need definitions for communications sciences, information sciences and documentation."[5] Here we see what may have been not only a saturation of the number of categories manageable by short term memory, but also the development or relationships between documentation and other communication-oriented disciplines of the same generation.

Information retrieval, a term introduced by Mooers in 1950, according to Fairthorne, denoted "the recovery from a given collection of documents, and with stated probability, of a set of documents that includes . . . all documents of a specified content. . . ."[6] But Fairthorne in 1961 went considerably beyond the topic of document retrieval through his inclusion of such topics as automata and self-organizing systems, linguistics, mathematics, and the theory of communication. Vickery also discussed information retrieval from a communications standpoint: "Retrieval is a form of communication and we may expect its analysis to be aided by other studies in the Communication Sciences."[7] Such observations mark a transition from the documentation paradigm to the information storage and retrieval paradigm and show a recognition of its relationship to the communication sciences.

In 1963 Becker and Hayes reported seven basic categories of information retrieval, through a content analysis of their own work, and emphasized the interdisciplinary communications character of the field.[8]

1. Human communication
2. Communication in Libraries
3. Organization of Information
4. Equipment
5. Intellect and cognition
6. Numerical measurement
7. Adaptation

Thus, from the standpoint of short-term memory limits, information retrieval appears to have developed

a numerically sufficient set of categories to display
attributes of a disciplinary system as early as 1963. In
1964 Borko and Doyle reported that information
retrieval, after a decade of sluggish development, was
starting to ascend from its equipment and gadget
orientation to higher levels of abstraction, which
denoted a trend toward fundamental science. Their
emphasis was divided equally between documentation
and communication and linguistic research. They
briefly noted the emergence of information science, "a
true interdisciplinary science involving the efforts of
librarians, logicians, linguists, engineers, mathematicians, and behavioral scientists."[9]

During the emergence and expansion of documentation and informational retrieval, simultaneous and similar trends could be discerned in the
behavioral and communication sciences. The close
chronological emergence of these fields, as discussed
in chapter 3, is again reviewed.

1933   Linguistics, Semantics
1938   Value Inquiry
1939   Decision Theory
1944   Game Theory
1945   Documentation
1948   Information Theory, Cybernetics
1950   General Systems Theory, Information
Retrieval
1950s   Communication and Behavioral Sciences
formed

As indicated earlier, the probability of the random but
simultaneous emergence of a group of concepts or dis-

ciplinary systems is indeed small. This suggests the interpretation that these fields emerged as specialized responses to the same or similar underlying problems, and that they are complementary if not duplicative of each other. Following their emergence around the time of World War II, the communication and behavioral sciences expanded in scope and started to interpenetrate.

The interpenetration of the behavioral and communications disciplines did not go unnoticed. Colin Cherry observed in 1957 the growth of similarity among the communications disciplines: "a certain unity of a group of studies is growing, originally diverse and disconnected but all related to our *communicative* activities."[10] Behavioral scientists, like the documentalists and information retrieval specialists, set out to "develop the sciences of information, classification, coding, storage, retrieval, supply and recycling of information."[11] Information theory had diffused rapidly through a large number of disciplines, including several of the contributory disciplines of information science.[12] The year 1957 was approximately the midpoint of a shift of attention in documentation from manual to computer based retrieval systems, thus bringing in a new focal point for the convergence of informational, behavioral, and communications disciplines.[13]

Efforts to find a common meeting ground continued. As early as 1956, a main objective of general systems theory was to develop "a framework of general theory to enable one specialist to catch relevant communications from others."[14] Cybernetics became popular throughout the world and particularly in the Soviet Union.

Cybernetics, essentially a unifying science, may have its most important influence in stimulating dialogue not only between the sciences and applied sciences, but, more importantly, between the sciences and the humanities. . . . the central concept in every one of the modern disciplines, sciences, and arts relates to pattern and configuration. . . . the development of patterns . . . involves the retrieval, analysis and synthesis of knowledge . . . there is an urgent need to classify and catalog knowledge in a way that will facilitate the establishment of structure.[15]

It was in this rather homogeneous disciplinary environment that information science emerged, and was defined in 1962 as

the science that investigates the properties and behavior of information, the forces governing the flow of information, and the means of processing information for optimum accessibility and usability. The processes include the origination, dissemination, collection, organization, storage, retrieval, interpretation, and use of information.[16]

In sum, information science emerged largely from its archetypes of documentation and information retrieval and in the midst of a maturing World War II generation of communications-convergent disciplines. Now let us take a look at where information science stands today.

Contemporary Views of Information Science

When information science came to be viewed as a basic area of inquiry, attempts to define the new field reached higher levels of abstraction. As of 1964, according to Wyllys, information retrieval had not attained the status of a scientific discipline, but was still very much an applied field; however, retrieval specialists had at least achieved the level at which they could discern the fundamental nature of their problem.[17] Wooster had observed in 1962 that an informational *science* was fundamental to the technological imperatives of information storage and retrieval. He described four functional areas of information science: (1) pattern recognition, (2) lexical processing, (3) decision-making, and (4) encoding for communications and control.[18] In 1964 Wooster redefined these areas to include (1) epistemology, (2) intelligent automata, (3) pattern recognition from visual to semantic, (4) self-organization, and (5) computer organization and programming.[19] By 1967 Wooster included the six areas of (1) information systems research, (2) information identification and classification, (3) information transmission, (4) adaptive and self-organizing systems, (5) language and linguistics research, and (6) theoretical foundations. He also reported reasonable progress toward the mechanization of inductive inference.[20]

Taylor observed in 1963 that the behavioral sciences provide a fundamental approach to information science, along with logic and mathematics, linguistics and systems analysis.[21] In this period similar behavioral developments could be noted in management science. Four movements gave rise to the design and operations of information systems for management decision-making: (1) behaviorally oriented studies of information transfer; (2) mathematics and statistics; (3) intra-organization data flow and systems analysis; and (4) scientific research methodology, including general systems theory.[22] The communication and behavioral science aspects of information science were thus becoming apparent. In general the relatively few definitive views of information science offered in the early 1960s tended to be circumspect and tentative. By 1967, however, relationships between information science and the communication sciences were more clearly discerned. Weisman argued, for example, that "information science is a basic and major component of communication."[23] In turn, he viewed the communication sciences as an interdisciplinary field, not a discipline, the concerns of which involve

> the multiple processes of communication and exchange of information by natural and artificial systems. Within its study are natural (human, animal and insect) and artificial languages (including codes used in communication systems, design languages, programming languages for computers and the formal language of mathematical logic) as modes of communication. Included are investigations of communications systems found in nature (organic and inorganic) and of machine automata as information processing systems.[24]

Gorn, in contrast, viewed information science as a "sharply defined discipline in its own right, rather than just another interdisciplinary area."[25] He tentatively labeled this discipline "Cybernetic Pragmatism," which in effect is a reformulation of the concept of liberal education.

> One which would place the arts, sciences, humanities, and professions in closer communication, possible even to the point of achieving agreement in general educational aims. It is itself part of a liberal arts contribution of this new discipline, as is an understanding of what can and what cannot be mechanized.[26]

Gorn saw a key role for information science in "interdisciplinary politics," including the establishment of community between the sciences and humanities. He emphasized that various disciplines possess several information science components: (1) principles of economy and simplicity; (2) processes or flows of events conditioned by the factor of memory; (3) stability or steady-state principles; (4) pressure and density principles; (5) transition or transformation; and (6) growth. These information science components, it might be noted, resemble the isomorphisms of general systems theory: "concepts such as wholeness and sum, mechanization, centralization, hierarchical order, stationary and steady states, equifinality, etc. are found in different fields. . . ."[27] Thus Gorn viewed information science essentially as an integrative discipline designed to cope with the "most serious interdisciplinary problem, namely the relationship of the arts and sciences to the professional schools."[28]

The growth of information science, Gorn argued, is like that of other disciplines and is influenced by memory limits.

When the domain of general information . . . passes its critical mass for the memory or retrieval device, either fission into subdomains or fusion into more compact structures occurs; that is, either fragmentation into separate disciplines occurs, or the revolution changes the structure of the discipline into the next phase in the development of a language system.[29]

Every discipline, in turn, may be regarded as "systems containing a communication subsystem and a control subsystem;"[30] when such communication or control subsystems reach a critical point, fission or fusion occurs to effect the reorganization of the system for continued growth. Growth and transformation occur until the discipline becomes a "full-fledged self-referencing" language system. The disciplines are thus comparable to growing organisms, which "change their outlines and subject matter in accordance with economy principles in the linguistic communication process."[31] Gorn's explanation, it would seem, provides an interpretation of the transitions from the earlier documentation and information retrieval paradigms to that of information science. Moreover, Gorn provides the cue that the information science paradigm is not necessarily permanent.

Slamecka has expressed a version of information science somewhat similar to Gorn's in that he embraces in one paradigm the basic as well as the pragmatic concerns of information science. According to Slamecka, information processes can be reduced essentially to sign or symbol manipulation from the perspectives of information theory, information processes, and information systems. With these areas of concern a true science of information would inquire into such areas as problem-solving, decision-making, forecasting, the codification of knowledge, research heuristics, and cognitive processes.[32]

In a 1968 paper Kochen appears to shy away from the information paradigm. He avoids heavy use of the term "information science" and renders a conservative delineation of the emerging disciplines of "epistemo-dynamics," which could form the nucleus of the information sciences. Epistemo-dynamics "is concerned with lawful regularities governing the acquisition of information and its transmission into knowledge, the assimilation of knowledge into understanding, the fusion of understanding into wisdom."[33] This discipline would require a fusion of the sciences and humanities, in addition to a scientific understanding of science itself. The topic of "research on research. . . . might well coalesce into the theoretical nucleus of information science. . . ."[34] But Kochen's central theme involves stochastic or growth processes, which can be applied to a wide variety of information phenomena—including the processes of learning and growth.

In 1969, Tosio Kitagawa, statistician and director of the Research Institute of Fundamental Information Science, Kyushu University, published a lengthy monograph on information science. His definition follows:

By information science we mean a newly organized branch of science. . . . it is presently drafting a form of blueprint of its own future development. . . . constituents range over a vast ensemble of individual sciences, and it . . . is an amalgamated science whose constituent branches have their respective scientific principles.[35]

Kitagawa proposed the following "five indispensable research branches" and research subdivisions as basic to the structure of information science:[36]

Branch 1. Physical information phenomena.

1.1 Metal and magnetic elements.
1.2 Semiconductor elements.
1.3 Cryogenic elements.
1.4 Optical information elements.
1.5 Fluid information elements.
1.6 Elastic wave information elements.
1.7 Chemical information elements.
1.8 Dielectric information elements.

Branch 2. Theoretical formulation of information phenomena.

2.1 Logic.
2.2 Theory of recognition.
2.3 Theory of linguistics.
2.4 Theory of information networks.
2.5 Self-organizing systems.
2.6 Learning theory.
2.7 Theory of information transmission.
2.8 Information theory.
2.9 Mathematical programming.
2.10 Statistical theory.

Branch 3. Information system analysis.

3.1   Information processing systems.
3.2   Computation systems.
3.3   Information control.
3.4   System analysis.
3.5   Man-machine systems.
3.6   Operational analysis.

Branch 4. Information phenomena in biological existence.

4.1   Neurophysiology.
4.2   Integration of the central nervous system.
4.3   Sensory information processing.
4.4   Transmission of genetic information.
4.5   Exhibition of genetic information.
4.6   Adjustment of genetic information.

Branch 5. Artificial realization of information phenomena.

5.1   Information circuits.
5.2   Information transmission apparata (trans-ducers).
5.3   Information transformation apparata.
5.4   Recognition apparata.
5.5   Language apparata.
5.6   Thinking apparata.
5.7   Adaptation apparata.
5.8   Education apparata.

Each branch contains from six to ten (an average

of 7.6) research subdivisions, which accords with the notion that groupings of knowledge tend to be restricted to cognitively manageable proportions.

Kitagawa emphasized the clear connection of information science with statistics, and strong interrelationships with the behavioral sciences—all of which have the "remarkable common tendency" toward model building. Other neighboring disciplines include cybernetics, bionics, mathematics, library science and documentation. Synoptically, Kitagawa views information science as an objective, subjective and practical area of inquiry, thus raising questions about whether or not the traditional "science" paradigm of information science is really appropriate with a subjective and practical emphasis, insofar as most conceptions of science emphasize objectivity and freedom from the constraints of pragmatism.

In summary, recent attempts to define information science, particularly since 1966, reveal close relationships with the historically contemporaneous behavioral and communication sciences, especially cybernetics, general and special systems theory, and decision-making. Information science appears to have grown to the point where its fundamental branches are emerging, though perhaps on a trial-and-error basis. In general, a period of unified but confused growth appears to be drawing to a close, which suggests an end to the era of the generalist in information science.

Future Development of Information Science

It may be recalled in Gorn's discussion that when a disciplinary system surpasses the limits of its memory, or critical mass, it either fragments into smaller, more compact units or its structure is reconstellated for the next phase of its development. Such a process appears to have occurred when the documentation and retrieval paradigms formed and transformed, eventually becoming instrumental in the reconstellation which resulted in information science. In general, the emergence, growth, and beginning differentiation of information science is not unlike the corresponding developmental phases of the older disciplines discussed in chapter 3.

Of the total period required for the emergence, growth, and differentiation of several disciplines reviewed in chapter 3, an average of 41 percent was required for emergence, 33 percent for early growth, and 26 percent for differentiation into specialized branches. Assuming that the formative period of documentation was approximately 50 years (1895 to 1945), and that the unified growth period was approximately 20 years (1945-1965), then approximately 74 percent of the time span would extend from 1895 to 1965. The total time span would then extend approximately 94 years beyond 1895, or to 1989. If this estimate is correct, information science will be fully mature, with pronounced specialization within its ranks, well before the end of this century.

The above projection is, however, only a crude approximation, since it is based on averages of nebulous developmental periods of older disciplines. Moreover, such a projection should not imply that further reconstellations of the present information science paradigm will not occur, or that the name of the discipline will not change. Gorn has used the term "cybernetic pragmatism" while Kochen discussed "epistemo-dynamics," thus providing cues of an impending restructuring or redesignation of the field.

In chapter 3 it was pointed out that disciplinary systems normally develop approximately seven branch subsystems, presumably as a reflection of man's tendency to restrict organizations of knowledge to cognitively convenient proportions. On the assumption that human short-term memory limitations will continue to be imposed on human organizations of knowledge, information science should develop into approximately seven specialized subsystems. In 1962 and 1964 Gorn described four subsystems of information science; in 1967 he included six. In 1969, Kitagawa described five branches. If such descriptions accurately reflect the rate of growth and present structure of information science, approximately two more subsystems could emerge in the early 1970s.

As noted earlier in this chapter, documentation expanded from three divisions in 1957 to nine in 1966, at which time the documentation paradigm began to be challenged by the information science paradigm. In a similar fashion, information science could expand from three divisions in 1962 to nine divisions in 1971, at which time the information science paradigm could be challenged by a newer one of more appropriate scope. However, Gorn observes that the second fusion of a discipline "permits considerably more compactness in the discipline's communication."[37] If information science represents the second or third fusion of the discipline, then any subsequent phase could be considerably more stable than the early documentation phase. It is during the first phase that the "nouns" of a new discipline are tentatively selected. A subsequent developmental phase of information science, according to Gorn's description, could involve a formalization of its basic concepts and eventually the establishment of stronger relationships with its neighboring disciplines.

> In summary, then, any discipline is concerned with the development of its own characteristic processes and concepts; these change with time as the people in the discipline change, pragmatically, their ideas as to what is worth perceiving and discussing in the discipline. In any event the discipline grows like a language system and develops linguistic processes which simulate the processes under consideration. Thus the disciplines are growing organisms which change their outlines in accordance with economy principles in the linguistic communication process. . . . when the population of information is thin, disciplines appear to be clusters as sharply separated as galaxies in the universe. As the population becomes denser, the lines of demarcation disappear. . . .[38]

The tendency for information science to become more like certain of the communication and behavioral sciences, and conversely, has already been discussed. In the previous chapter it was seen that disciplinary members of the social science sub-suprasystem interpenetrated during a final maturation and synthesis phase. The integrative disciplines might also be expected to integrate themselves with one another, in a manner analogous to the way in which adjacent but well-separated trees grow into a thick forest and later into a jungle.

Kitagawa has suggested that "we should be conscious of the laws governing birth, growth and death of a science and we should have a 'medical plan' which is effective throughout the entire life of a science."[39] A similar concept has arisen in psychology.

> Those persons and institutions engaged in the production, communication and use of psychological knowledge constitute a *dynamic system* in which events occurring in any one part are reflected in other elements of the system and ultimately in the performance of the discipline.[40]

Accordingly, psychologists would be expected to examine the system's performance as it serves the needs of science and society, to understand its functioning and to exercise appropriate management of it. A programmed development of the system would impose the need to

1. describe the functioning of the total system and its components;
2. identify the leverage points;
3. identify the potential forms of leverage;
4. provide an appropriate goal-setting and decision-making apparatus;
5. provide an effective operations apparatus.[41]

Although issues are bound to arise concerning the degree to which a discipline should be "managed" or permitted "naturally" to evolve, certain possible future roles for information science may be discussed. Becker and Hayes have regarded "a total scientific discipline as analogous to an information system."[42] To the extent that information science is a complete or total system, and is appropriately organized, it can serve its explanatory and heuristic purposes.

One task which could possibly further the completeness and internal development of information science would be the addition of needed subsystem components. Several possible additional subsystems were discussed in the previous section, including general systems theory, forecasting, and a science of research. The development of a science of research is particularly interesting in that the term "science information" has been confused with "information science."[43] Perhaps this confusion is somewhat justified since the distinction between science and research can be confused, and a "science of research" could be an intrinsic but latent part of information science. In 1959, Tykociner drew a distinction between research, the striving for new knowledge, and science, "the sum total of recorded, systematized knowledge thus far accumulated by the human race."[44] Tykociner also proposed a science of research. Hoshovsky and Massey have proposed that a fundamental task of information science is to promote the juxtaposition of problems and useful data within the human mind in order that productive unions take place in support of decision-making.[45] But other additions, besides a science of research, could be important to the development of information science. The problem of "what is missing" in information science awaits resolution. Moreover, the question of whether information science in its present form will survive is yet to be decided.

In addition to its self-development, information science might be concerned with outside developmental and integrative tasks aimed toward the communication and behavioral sciences and other large systems within a potentially emerging suprasystem of knowledge. In short, information science could catalyze the formation of a suprasystem through:

1. the penetration and development of other communication sciences to form a viable communication sub-suprasystem;
2. use of the communication sub-suprasystem to integrate the humanities, sciences and professions; and
3. support of the emergence of new sub-suprasystems which are requisite to the formation of a suprasystem.

Last, information scientists might well be concerned with ways to overcome the debilitating effects of human short-term memory in problem-solving. Hunter points out that failure to solve problems is often attributable to over-heavy demands on short-term memory.

> The solving of a complex problem in, say, scientific research involves novel combinations of ideas, that is . . . of unaccustomed relationships. Now this coherent pattern may comprize a large number of component relationships which must . . . be brought to mind together and at nearly the same time. Such holding together of components—comprehending—requires the collective recalling of the components . . . the activity of comprehending may well be limited by short term memory.[46]

To arrive at a point where comprehension is possible

usually requires long preliminary labor. Presumably a task of information science is to ease the burden of comprehension. But whether truly synoptic comprehension is humanly possible remains an open question.

Summary

Information science appears to have emerged not only as an expression and metamorphosis of documentation and information retrieval; it directly or indirectly incorporated or paralleled several prevailing objectives and concepts of the communication and behavioral sciences and other contributory disciplines. The communication and behavioral sciences emerged with documentation and from the outset apparently shared many of its problems. The formative pattern of documentation resembles that of other disciplinary systems.

Information science was initially defined in 1962, and has since been characterized as a fundamental science. Its unified growth appears to be ending and fundamental branches are emerging. Information science, as well as documentation and information retrieval, have been identified as communication disciplines. Recent attempts to define information science suggest links with the communication and behavioral sciences. In the early 1970s information science will possibly be complete as a disciplinary system. By 1990, it should have achieved a relative state of maturity; specialization within its ranks could become intense. But new fusions and fissions, with attendant name changes, could occur within the next two decades.

The development of information science might be

programmed to include new areas such as the science of research, which possibly exists as a latent component of information science. A potential long-range role for information science involves active participation in forming a complete suprasystem of knowledge that could unify the arts, sciences, and professions. Finally, information science could strive to overcome the limitations of human memory and thereby increase the scope of human comprehension.

6

Conclusion

This chapter recapitulates the previous chapters, draws together some loose ends, and suggests a few implications. Before summarizing, it must be pointed out that immense and complex areas of inquiry have been covered. It is not difficult to raise objections to the occasional superficial treatment of many of these areas, or to the relatively singular approach to a topic which might call for myriad approaches. It should be stressed that approaches other then the systems approach used herein could, for various purposes and values, prove to be quite informative. Von Laue states that "history can be written from quite divergent viewpoints but still with complete adherence to the truth."[1] No attempt has been made to pre-empt or overturn viewpoints—at least not untactfully. One measure of the success of this work is the extent to which it sharpens divergent viewpoints or differences in underlying values and assumptions.

A considerable degree of simplification is apparent in this report, particularly in the representation of complex phenomena through the use of linear landmark chronologies. The following rationale, employed by Hardin, is perhaps applicable here:

History is not a chain of discrete events laid out like beads on a chain. There is a tremendous

amount of temporal overlap of different processes in the development of both ideas and institu-
tions. The total reality of history is so rich in detail
that we cannot gain a complete knowledge of the
past without sacrificing our own lives. Therefore,
we simplify . . . rather than entirely give up our
efforts to understand. . . .[2]

In general, I have favored the approach of David
Easton, who has asserted that "concepts are neither
true nor false; they are more or less useful."[3] The concepts of general systems theory were employed in this
inquiry for their analytical value. Their extensive use
heightens the possibility that systematic attributes will
be subjectively imposed on phenomena which are not
empirically systematic, at least not as imagined by
systems-oriented subjectivists. But I have tried to high-
light this subjectivist tendency by pointing out that
short-term memory limitations have often forced
humans not only to adopt systematic concepts, but to
adopt concepts which are drastically restricted in depth
as well as in breadth. The construction of conceptual
systems, whether in the rational, empirical, or
pragmatic areas, appears to be an essential step toward
conceptual economy; conceptual economy appears to
be a requisite for complex human cognitive operations.

To summarize the approach and findings, the key
objective of this work was to explore relationships
between the formation of disciplinary systems and
human memory limitations. In so doing, it emphasizes
the apparent tendency of humans to produce well-
circumscribed organizations of knowledge which
reflect their own memory limitations. Although infor-

mation science is the focal discipline of this inquiry, the formative patterns of other disciplines, particularly mathematics and physics are interpreted. In addition, the development of systematic groups of disciplines are considered as a prelude to discussing the potential emergence of a comprehensive suprasystem of human knowledge.

Methodological problems abound in an inquiry so extensive as this one. In general, the work interprets the chronological emergence of various disciplines and develops a common formative pattern. The selection of these disciplines was based primarily on an assessment of their potential in elucidating the origins and development of information science. Cases in mathematics and physics were selected because their histories are reasonably well documented. Equivalent historical perspective is not available for disciplines which have emerged more recently, particularly those which are contemporaneous with information science. But an analysis of such recent disciplines was conducted to point out apparent similarities between modern disciplines.

In order to minimize the influence of my own biases, the interpretations and consensus of two or more historians were used to construct chronologies representing the formation and transformation of disciplinary subsystems, systems, and suprasystems. I have also relied rather heavily on the interpretations of historians of science to discern relationships between formative patterns and human memory limits. Similarities in the formative and developmental patterns of the several disciplinary systems studied, led to the development of a quantitative method to analyze and predict the developmental patterns of other disciplines. Again,

to minimize the influence of my own biases, this predictive method was tested on chronologies constructed
by persons other than myself. In the cases analyzed,
it can be noted that approximately seven ideas
coalesced to form disciplinary sub-subsystems or subsystems; seven subsystems coalesced to form a disciplinary system; seven disciplinary systems coalesced to
form a group or sub-suprasystem of disciplines.
Furthermore, these suprasystems have historically
tended to consist of seven sub-suprasystems. The
number seven is, of course, only approximate. But it
is manifest in the length of sentences and syllogistic
chains, and in the hierarchic spans of subdisciplines,
disciplines and supradisciplines. These tendencies for
man-made groupings of knowledge to consist of seven
components can possibly be explained by the fact that
human short-term memory can effectively span only
about seven items.

In the cases studied, such disciplinary groupings
and regroupings appeared to be periodic and hence
somewhat predictable. Synthesis tended to occur when
approximately seven ideas were available for synthesis,
often in the form of a relatively independent, simultaneous discovery. If one investigator did not effect a
needed synthesis, another would, presumably because
syntheses were often conceptually elegant and essential
to the progress of inquiry. As the limits of human
short-term memory were threatened or surpassed by
an accumulation of unordered findings, systematization was apparently necessary for any further inquiries
based on recall of past inquiries. In turn, as the
number of contributions or syntheses along a given
line of inquiry became too numerous for scientists to
remember, these contributions or syntheses were sys-

tematized to form a discipline. The subsequent growth
and transformation of each discipline involved increasing specialization within its own ranks, again a condition presumably influenced by fixed human cognitive
limitations. Disciplines appear to be organized primarily for cognitive manageability, and secondarily for
adequacy in other respects.

Four contemporary groups of disciplines or sub-
suprasystems—the humanities, physical science, biological sciences, and social sciences—emerged somewhat
successively but with considerable temporal overlapping. What appears to be a fifth, integrative sub-
suprasystem has emerged in the form of the communication or behavioral sciences. The behavioral and communication disciplines emerged at approximately the
same time, which suggests their origin in a common
problem. The communication and behavioral sciences
show signs of converging toward at least one common
aim—the integration of the arts, sciences, and professions. Should existing sub-suprasystems integrate with
one another, the formation of a comprehensive suprasystem of knowledge might be expected. This suprasystem could assume several forms but would to
some extent be a codification of existing knowledge as
it would unify existing groups of disciplines and incor-
porate newly emergent generations of disciplines.
Further, a suprasystem could require or result in the
encyclopedic reduction, synthesis and systematization
of knowledge—possibly in the form of a world brain
or encyclopedia. Such a suprasystem could form within
the next one hundred years.

Information science emerged from its archetypes
of documentation and information storage and
retrieval, and from other computer and information-

oriented contributory disciplines. Thus, information science appears to be a member of a set of communication-oriented disciplines which emerged almost simultaneously around World War II. The evolution of relationships between information science and other members of its generation of disciplines indicates a trend toward commonality and unity. But it should be emphasized that further transformations of information science can be expected. The information paradigm, derived primarily from the Shannon and Weaver information theory, is of course subject to challenge and possible replacement by a paradigm with a more appropriate locus and scope. Even if the information paradigm does prove to be durable, it would not necessarily be sheltered from the influences which have subdivided, fragmented, and otherwise transformed other disciplines. These same remarks might well apply to the "science" paradigm portion of information science.

To some extent the future of information science could be actively programmed. Information science and other communication-oriented disciplines could serve to form a suprasystem of knowledge potentially capable of unifying the arts, sciences and professions. Such a suprasystem or "world brain" could provide a basis for a more complete interpretation of reality. It would appear that the complex population-resource-environmental problems which the world faces, or is about to face, cannot be adequately defined by our present disjointed system of knowledge, marked by its gulfs between the sciences and humanities and between theoretical and pragmatic fields.

The confrontation of extraordinarily pervasive contemporary problems will require a correspondingly comprehensive system of knowledge. Such a comprehensive system of knowledge would far exceed the limited grasp of individual human memories. In brief: information science might well be devoted to the task of forming a comprehensive suprasystem of knowledge and to the further provision of means by which human comprehension could exceed the constraints of short term memory.

There are, of course, other factors besides memory which can influence the formation of disciplines. In the concentrated enthusiasm and treatment of the memory theme I have been a narrow specialist. The main purpose was to point out the tendency of humans to produce well-circumscribed organizations of knowledge which apparently reflect their own memory limitations. However, memory might not be the decisive influence.

An infinite number of other hypotheses can be advanced to explain the phenomenon of disciplinary formation. For example, one might assume that each contribution in any particular topic might reduce uncertainly by some fraction, say one-half. If so, the first contribution would reduce the entire area of uncertainty by one-half. The second contribution would explain one-half of the unexplained remainder, or one-quarter of the total topic. The third contribution would again reduce the remaining area of uncertainty by one-half, or the total initial area of uncertainty by one-eighth, and so on. After the seventh contribution, the remaining area of uncertainty would be extremely small. In a way analogous to Zeno's paradox, that remaining area of uncertainty would never be totally eliminated by additional contributions. Uncertainty would merely be reduced and the inquiry would thus remain forever open-ended. This reduction-of-uncertainty hypothesis could serve as one of an infinite number of alternative hypotheses to my memory hypothesis.

This hypothesis needs further qualification. At the present, we know relatively little about the true nature of short-term memory. The great bulk of research on this topic has been carried out only since 1959, and short-term memory continues to be a topic of intense empirical investigation.[4] Although few definitive conclusions about short-term memory can be stated at this time, G. A. Miller's insight that it can embrace approximately seven items has stood the test of time.[5] Deutsch points out that human information processing is best supported when categorical groups and subgroups consist of no more than about seven members.[6] Nevertheless, the economic relationships between short-term and long-term memory have yet to clearly be worked out. J. G. Miller states several interesting hypotheses about memory which differentiate between short-term memory and the general human capacity to process information.[7] There possibly exists some inverse relationship between memory size or depth of storage and recall accuracy or access time. If this speculation is correct, there can be either high-speed information processing with a relatively accurate and low-capacity memory or, conversely, slow or possibly less accurate processing and high-capacity memory. Thus, human short-term memory might be somewhat analogous to a computer's low-capacity but speedy working memory, while long-term memory could be analogous to the computer's more cumbersome and slower high-capacity memory.[8] In sum, it was argued here that discoveries and disciplinary syntheses tend to bear the strong imprint of human short-term memory. Admittedly, the precise nature of human memory is still quite controversial. If our notions of human memory were to be radically changed, the arguments put forth here would require revision.

One debate in the history of science is whether science is an evolutionary or revolutionary development. Kuhn, for example, has viewed the transformation of knowledge as a revolutionary process. Once a paradigm is erected, "mopping-up operations are what engage most scientists throughout their careers."[9] It requires a career of revolt on the part of other scientists to replace or establish the paradigm. To Kuhn, however, a revolution need not involve a dramatic crisis, but would merely be a special class of change involving a reconstruction of group commitments among the community of scientists. Revolutions, then, supply "a self-correcting mechanism which ensures that the rigidity of science will not forever go unchallenged."[10]

In general, a position of eclecticism was adopted with regard to the nature of scientific development. Nevertheless, the various cases which have been presented tend to be an evolutionary interpretation of the growth and transformation of disciplines. When a sufficient number of contributions accumulates, a "systems man" or group of men organizes these contributions in a novel way to form what Kuhn calls a paradigm. The distribution of contributions was viewed along the time scale in a prospective or future-oriented manner. That is, each landmark contribution was viewed as pre-paradigm, leading to some sort of culminating synthesis. So, for the purpose of predicting discoveries or synthesis, the evolutionary approach was chosen.

On the other hand, a retrospective or past-oriented approach might have been adopted. Many of the landmark contributions which were used as illustration could have been viewed as post-paradigm, or as attempts to overthrow or drastically modify some previously established paradigm. Such a retrospective, post-paradigm approach might have been viewed as revolutionary. But, to repeat, one of the purposes was to predict discoveries or disciplinary synthesis. For this end, a prospective orientation proved more valuable than a retrospective orientation. This should not imply that retrospective orientations lack predictive value.

Perhaps the evolutionary-revolutionary debate should be raised to a higher level of abstraction, in order to permit the evolutionary and revolutionary aspects of scientific development to be seen as special cases of something more general. If a scientific discovery D is modeled as a complete, ordered set of approximately seven informational elements, D {a, b, c, d, e, f, g,}, then one might assume that at different time points before or after the discovery, the set of elements would be either numerically insufficient or sufficient. Further, these elements would be basically unordered or ordered. Hence the formation of a new paradigm, using the evolutionary approach, would involve the acquisition and ordering of information elements until a relatively complete and orderly new paradigm is formed. Using a revolutionary approach, information elements would be accumulated against an old paradigm in an attempt to reorder or replace the old paradigm. But the very same contributions could be accumulated simultaneously against an old paradigm and toward a new paradigm. Hence, the very same line of inquiry would be simultaneously revolutionary and evolutionary.

Goffman and I have used this information element model to predict discoveries in the field of symbolic logic, and the reader is referred to our published work for a fuller discussion.[11] In short, the evolutionary-revolutionary debate might well be viewed in less dichotomous, more generalized terms. Both evolutionary and revolutionary scientific development might be viewed as special instances of system formation and transformation.

In closing, it should be stressed that this inquiry has attempted to deal with only one of possibly hundreds of identifiable variables which could influence the formation of disciplinary systems. The potential contribution of this inquiry is the insight that memory limitations do influence human organizations of knowledge.

Appendix

**Summary Portion of F. S. Soddy's 1921
Nobel Award Address (© Nobel Foundation 1922)**

We may now sum up the various distinct steps in this long and tangled story of the origins of the conception and discovery of isotopes.

1. Experimental methods are available, uniquely for the radio-elements, which enable isotopes to be severally recognized, by a suitable combination of chemical analyses at appropriate intervals of time, whereby, owing to the successive changes of the constituents, they may be separated, although chemical analysis alone is quite unable to effect this separation. This dates from 1905.
2. The complete chemical identity of isotopes, as distinct from close chemical similarity, came gradually to be recognized. McCoy and Ross were the first to express a definite opinion in this sense (1907).
3. The existence of chemical identities among the radio elements led to the deduction that they might exist among the common elements and be responsible for the exceptions in the Periodic classification, and for the fact that the atomic weights in some cases depart widely from integral values. Ströholm and Svedberg first made this deduction (1909).
4. The recognition of the effect of the explusion of, first, the α-and then, the β-particle (1911 and 1913) led to the correct placing of all three disintegration series

from end to end in the Periodic Table. On the experimental side the names of A. Fleck, and on the theoretical side that of G. von Hevesy and A. S. Russell, but pre-eminently that of Kasimir Fajans, are associated with this advance.

5. The identity of isotopes was extended to include their electro-chemistry (Paneth and Hevesy) and their spectra (Russell and Rossi), though here infinitesimal differences were subsequently found (Harkins and Aronberg, Merton). [Ca. 1913]

6. Isotopes, on Rutherford's theory of atomic pressure, are elements with identical external electronic systems, with identical net positive charge on the nucleus, but with nuclei in which the total number of positive and negative charges and therefore the mass is different. The originator of the view that the places in the Periodic Table correspond with unit difference of intra-atomic charge is Van den Broek. [1911]

7. Moseley extended this view to the non-radioactive elements, and ultimately for the whole Periodic Table, and the definite determination of the number and sequence of the places in it became possible. [1913]

8. The chemistry of the radioactive elements and the lacunae previously existing in the radioactive series, especially in connection with the origin of actinium, have been cleared up, and this led to the discovery of a new element, proto-actinium (eka-tantalum) in uranium minerals, occupying the place between uranium and thorium and existing in sufficient quantity for the compounds of the element to be prepared in a pure state, and its spectrum and atomic weight ultimately to be determined, as Mme. Curie did for radium. Cranston and I share with Hahn and Meitner the original discovery, but the subsequent developments are due to the latter.

9. The preparation from radioactive minerals of differ-

ent isotopes of lead followed and the determination of their atomic weight, spectrum, density and other properties, established that the same chemical character and atomic volume can coexist with differences of atomic weight. The work on the ionium-thorium mixture from pitchblende is a second example.

10. The last result, and perhaps the most important of all, is the subject of the award of the Nobel Prize for Chemistry for 1922.

Notes

Chapter 1

[1] Jesse H. Shera, *Libraries and the Organization of Knowledge* (Hamden, Conn.: Archon Books, 1965), p. 14.

[2] Colin Cherry, *On Human Communication* (New York: John Wiley and Sons, Inc., 1957), p. 1.

[3] Robert Collison, *Encyclopedias: Their History Throughout the Ages* (New York: Hafner Publishing Company, 1964), pp. 82-100.

[4] R. J. Harvey-Gibson, *Two Thousand Years of Science* (New York: The Macmillan Company, 1931), p. 471. The term "invisible college" has been revived and popularized by Derek J. de Solla Price, *Science Since Babylon* (New Haven, Conn.: Yale University Press, 1961), pp. 54, 59, and in his other works.

[5] Floyd W. Matson, *The Broken Image: Man, Science and Society* (Garden City, N. Y.: Doubleday and Company, Inc., 1964), pp. 3-15.

[6] Joseph R. Royce, *The Encapsulated Man* (Princeton, N. J.: D. Van Nostrand Company, Inc., 1964), p. 37.

[7] Percy W. Bridgman, "Philosophical Implications of Physics," American Academy of Arts and Sciences, *Bulletin* 3 (February 1950), 136.

[8] George Schlesinger, *Method in the Physical Sciences* (New York: The Humanities Press, 1963), pp. 2-7, 8-12.

[9] Vannevar Bush, *Science Is Not Enough* (New York: William Morrow and Company, 1967), p. 28.

[10] Alvin M. Weinberg, *Reflections on Big Science* (Cambridge, Mass.: M.I.T. Press, 1967), p. 42.

[11] Kenneth Boulding, "General Systems Theory - The Skeleton of Science," *General Systems,* First Yearbook of the Society for General Systems Research (Ann Arbor, Mich.: Society for General Systems Research, 1956), p. 12.

[12] Bush, *Science Is Not Enough,* p. 92.

[13] John von Neuman, *The Computer and the Brain* (New Haven, Conn.: Yale University Press, 1958), p. 50.

[14] George A. Miller, "The Magical Number Seven, Plus or Minus Two: Some Limits on Our Capacity for Processing Information," *Psychological Review* 63 (March 1956), 81-97. Excerpts are drawn from pp. 82-95. Reprinted with supplementary writings in George A. Miller, *The Psychology of Communication: Seven Essays* (New York: Basic Books, Inc., 1967), pp. 14-44.

[15] Allen Newell and Herbert A. Simon, "Overview: Memory and Process in Concept Formation," in Benjamin Kleinmuntz (ed.), *Concepts and the Structure of Memory* (New York: John Wiley and Sons, Inc., 1967), pp. 241-262.

[16] Victor H. Yngve, "A Model and an Hypothesis for Language Structure," *Proceedings of the American Philosophical Society* 104 (October 1960), 452.

[17] Walter R. Reitman, *Cognition and Thought: An Information Processing Approach* (New York: John Wiley and Sons, Inc., 1965), p. 91.

[18] George A. Kelly, *The Psychology of Personal Constructs,* Vol. I: *A Theory of Personality* (New York: W. W. Norton and Company, Inc., 1965), p. 91.

[19] Milic Capek, "Ernst Mach's Biological Theory of Knowledge," *Synthese* 18 (April 1968), 191.

[20] Niels Bohr, *Atomic Physics and Human Knowledge* (New York: Science Editions, Inc., 1961), pp. 67-68.

[21] Herbert A. Simon, "The Architecture of Complexity," *General Systems,* Tenth Yearbook of the Society for

General Systems Research (Ann Arbor, Mich.: Society for General Systems Research, 1965), p. 71.

[22] Definitions are adapted from those of Oran R. Young, "A Survey of General Systems Theory," *General Systems*, Ninth Yearbook of the Society for General Systems Research (Ann Arbor, Mich.: Society for General Systems Research, 1964), 61-80. The definition of short term memory is from Ian M. L. Hunter, *Memory* (Baltimore: Penguin Books, 1964), p. 56.

Chapter 2

[1] George Sarton, *The Study of the History of Mathematics* (New York: Dover Publications, Inc., 1936), p. 20.

[2] Ibid., p. 9.

[3] Eric T. Bell, *The Development of Mathematics* (New York: McGraw-Hill Book Company, Inc., 1945), pp. 71-72.

[4] David E. Smith, *History of Mathematics,* Vol. I: *General Survey of the History of Mathematics* (Boston: Ginn and Company, 1925), pp. 55-107; W. W. Rouse Ball, *A Primer of the History of Mathematics* (London: Macmillan and Co., Limited, 1927), pp. 2-20; Dirk K. Struik, *A Concise History of Mathematics,* 3rd rev. ed., (New York: Dover Publications, Inc., 1967), pp. 37-65.

[5] Ball, Ibid., specifies which book of the *Elements* incorporated each prior contribution.

[6] Struik, *History of Mathematics,* p. 100.

[7] Ibid., p. 109.

[8] Smith, *History of Mathematics,* Vol. II, p. 701.

[9] Glenn James, *The Tree of Mathematics* (Arroyo Grande, Calif.: Digest Press, 1957), iv-viii.

[10] Simon, "Architecture of Complexity," p. 76.

[11] Derek T. Whiteside, ed., *The Mathematical Papers of Isaac Newton,* Vol.I: 1664-1666 (Cambridge, Mass: Cambridge University Press, 1967), p. 154. By permission.

[12] The ability to extrapolate information is discussed by Jerome S. Bruner, "On Perceptual Readiness," *Psychological Review* 64 (May 1957), 150-153.

[13] Henri Poincaré, "Mathematical Creation," *The Creative Process*, edited by Brewster Ghiselin (Berkeley: University of California Press, 1952), p. 34.

[14] Whiteside, *Mathematical Papers of Isaac Newton*, Vol. I, pp. 406-410.

[15] Smith, *History of Mathematics*, Vol. II, chap. x; Struik, *History of Mathematics*, chap. vii; Carl B. Boyer, *A History of Mathematics* (New York: John Wiley and Sons, Inc., 1968), pp. 404-452.

[16] Peter Caws, "Science and System: On the Unity and Diversity of Scientific Theory," *General Systems*, Thirteenth Yearbook of Society for General Systems Research (Ann Arbor, Mich.: Society for General Systems Research, 1968), p. 9.

[17] Louis T. More, *Isaac Newton: A Biography* (New York: Scribner's Sons, Inc., 1934), pp. 282-285; Florian Cajori, *A History of Physics*, rev. ed., (New York: Dover Publications, Inc., 1929), pp. 63-69.

[18] Bell, *Development of Mathematics*, pp. 443-448.

[19] From Smith, *History of Mathematics*, Vol. II, pp. 335-338; Boyer, *History of Mathematics*, pp. 572-594: Howard Eves, *An Introduction to the History of Mathematics* (New York: Rinehart and Company, Inc., 1953), pp. 122-126.

[20] R. J. Harvey-Gibson, *Two Thousand Years of Science*, 2d ed., (New York: Macmillan Company, 1931), p. 176.

[21] Owen W. Richardson, "Thermionic Phenomena: Laws Which Govern Them," in Nobel Foundation, *Nobel Lectures: Physics 1922-1941* (Amsterdam, Netherlands: Elsevier Publishing Company, 1965), pp. 224-225.

[22] Wolfgang Pauli, "Exclusion Principle and Quantum Mechanics," in Nobel Foundation, *Nobel Lectures: Physics 1942-1962* (Amsterdam, Netherlands: Elsevier Publishing Company, 1964), p. 29.

[23] Percentages are round figures. The 1675 date for discovery of the calculus is a half-way date between the discoveries of Newton and Leibniz.

[24] Garrett Hardin, *Biology: Its Principles and Implications,* 2d ed., (San Francisco: W. H. Freeman and Company, 1966), p. 637.

[25] Frederick Soddy, "The Origins of the Conceptions of Isotopes," in Nobel Foundation, *Nobel Lectures: Chemistry 1901-1921* (Amsterdam, Netherlands: Elsevier Publishing Company, 1966), pp. 371-399. © Nobel Foundation, 1922.

[26] B. M. Kedrov, "Toward a Methodological Analysis of Scientific Discoveries," *The Soviet Review* 4 (Spring 1963), 60-71.

[27] Hornell Hart, "Social Theory and Social Change," in Llewellyn Gross, ed., *Symposium on Sociological Theory* (Evanston, Ill.: Row, Peterson and Company, 1959), pp. 208-209.

[28] Gordon Tullock, *The Organization of Inquiry* (Durham, N. C.: Duke University Press, 1966), pp. 14, 100.

[29] George Schwartz and Philip W. Bishop, *Moments of Discovery,* Vol. I: *The Origins of Science* (New York: Basic Books, 1958), ix.

[30] Derek J. de Solla Price, *Little Science, Big Science* (New York: Columbia University Press, 1963), p. 78.

[31] "A Testimonial from Professor Einstein," in Jacques Hadamard, *The Psychology of Invention in the Mathematical Field* (New York: Dover Publications, Inc., 1945), Appendix II, pp. 142-143.

[32] Excerpt of lecture quoted in Hadamard, *Psychology of Invention in the Mathematical Field,* pp. 86-87.

Chapter 3

[1] See Harvey-Gibson, *Two Thousand Years of Science,* pp. 24-220, and Struik, *History of Mathematics,* pp. 99-182.

[2] Bonifari M. Kedrov, "Toward the Methodological

Analysis of Scientific Discoveries," *The Soviet Review* 4 (Spring 1963), 60.

[3] Edward G. Boring, *A History of Experimental Psychology*, 2d ed., (New York: Appleton-Century-Crofts, Inc., 1950), pp. 737-745.

[4] William Goffman and Vaun A. Newill, "Generalization of Epidemic Theory: an Application to the Transmission of Ideas," *Nature* 204 (October 17, 1964), 225-228. Simultaneous discovery is also discussed by Price, *Little Science, Big Science*, pp. 65-74.

[5] Bell, *Development of Mathematics*, p. 132.

[6] William Mendenhall, *Introduction to Probability and Statistics*, 2d ed., (Belmont, Calif.: Wadsworth Publishing Company, Inc., 1967), p. 66.

[7] Bell, *Development of Mathematics*, p. 134; Struik, *History of Mathematics*, p. 117.

[8] Struik, *History of Mathematics*, p. 140.

[9] Ibid., p. 174.

[10] James, *Tree of Mathematics*, iv.

[11] Derek J. de Solla Price, *Science Since Babylon* (New Haven, Conn.: Yale University Press, 1961), p. 68.

[12] Sources for outlines are, respectively, Bell, *Development of Mathematics*, pp. 132-166; W. W. Rouse Ball, *A Short Account of the History of Mathematics* (Cambridge: Cambridge University Press, 1888), pp. 411-445; René Taton, ed., *History of Science*, Vol. IV: *Science in the Twentieth Century*, trans. by A. J. Pomerans (New York: Basic Books, 1964), pp. 3-73.

[13] Raymond L. Wilder, *Evolution of Mathematical Concepts: An Elementary Study* (New York: John Wiley and Sons, Inc., 1968), pp. 207-209.

[14] Bell, *Development of Mathematics*, pp. 19, 34.

[15] Price, *Science Since Babylon*, p. 70.

[16] Max Von Laue, *History of Physics* (New York: Academic Press Inc., 1950), pp. 15-42, 97; Cajori, *A History of Physics*, pp. 57-105; Harvey-Gibson, *Two Thousand Years of Science*, pp. 41-49, 105-164.

[17] Price, *Little Science, Big Science,* p. 70.

[18] Von Laue, *History of Physics,* pp. 14-80.

[19] Gerhard A. Blass, *Theoretical Physics* (New York: Appleton-Century-Crofts, 1962), v.

[20] W. Wallace McCormick, *Fundamentals of College Physics* (New York: The Macmillan Company, 1964), iv.

[21] René Taton, ed., *History of Science,* Vol. II: *The Beginnings of Modern Science* (New York: Basic Books, Inc., 1958), p. 329; Taton, ed., vol. III: *Science in the Nineteenth Century* (New York: Basic Books, Inc., 1961), pp. 269, 285, 302; Taton, ed., Vol. IV: *Science in the Twentieth Century* (New York: Basic Books, Inc., 1964), pp. 251-285. Works trans. by A. J. Pomerans.

[22] Charles Singer, *A Short History of Scientific Ideas* (Oxford, England: Clarendon Press, 1959), pp. 382-384.

[23] Taton, ed., Vol. II: *Modern Science,* p. 369; Vol. III: *Nineteenth Century,* p. 376; Vol. IV: *Twentieth Century,* p. 312.

[24] Jerome S. Bruner and Gordon W. Allport, "Fifty Years of Change in American Psychology," *Psychological Bulletin* 38 (December 1940), 757-776.

[25] Cherry, *On Human Communication,* pp. 2-3.

[26] Lee Thayer, ed., *Communication: Concepts and Perspectives* (Washington, D. C.: Spartan Books, 1967), iii, p. 421.

[27] Sources are Cherry, *On Human Communication,* xi-xiv, and Thayer, ed., *Communication,* p. 427.

[28] Franz Alexander and others, "Behavioral Science: a New Journal," *Behavioral Science* 1 (January 1956), 2.

[29] Rollo Handy and Paul Kurtz, eds., *A Current Appraisal of the Behavioral Sciences* (Great Barrington, Mass.: Behavioral Research Council, 1964), pp. 97-141. Originally published as supplements to *The American Behavioral Scientist* 7 (September 1963 through March 1964), Sections 1-7.

[30] Ibid., p. 9.

[31] Ibid., p. 5.

[32] "The ABS Program," *The American Behavioral Scientist* 7 (November 1964), 60.

[33] Norbert Wiener, *The Human Use of Human Beings: Cybernetics and Society* (Garden City, New York: Doubleday and Company, Inc., 1954), p. 16.

[34] Norbert Wiener, *I Am a Mathematician* (Garden City, New York: Doubleday and Company, Inc., 1956), pp. 323-324.

[35] Claude E. Shannon and Warren Weaver, *The Mathematical Theory of Communication* (Urbana: University of Illinois Press, 1949), pp. 3-53.

[36] Colin Cherry, ed., *Information Theory: Proceedings of the Fourth London Symposium on Information Theory, 1960* (London: Butterworth, 1961), vii-ix.

[37] Oran R. Young, "Survey of General Systems Theory," *General Systems,* Ninth Yearbook, 61-62.

[38] Alfred Korzybski, *Science and Sanity,* 4th ed., (Lakeville, Conn.: International Non-Aristotelian Library Publishing Company, 1958), p. 376.

[39] Taton, ed., Vol. II: *Modern Science,* p. 9.

[40] Ibid.

[41] Von Laue, *History of Physics,* p. 4.

[42] Taton, ed., Vol. III: *Nineteenth Century,* p. 2.

[43] Price, *Science Since Babylon,* p. 70.

[44] Taton, ed., Vol. III: *Nineteenth Century,* p. 3, C. Moraze quoted.

[45] Price, *Little Science, Big Science,* p. 89.

[46] A. E. E. McKenzie, *The Major Achievements of Science,* Vol. I (Cambridge: Cambridge University Press, 1960), pp. 360-361.

[47] Herbert A. Simon, Donald W. Smithburg and Victor A. Thompson, *Public Administration* (New York: Alfred A. Knopf, 1959), pp. 131-132.

[48] Ibid., pp. 130-179.

[49] Edna Heidbreder, *Seven Psychologies* (New York: Appleton-Century-Crofts, Inc., 1933), ix; John E. Bentley, *Philosophy: An Outline-History* (Totowa, New Jersey: Littlefield Adams and Co., 1967), p. 146; Harry E. Barnes, *A

History of Historical Writing (Norman: University of Oklahoma Press, 1937), pp. 357-360; Abraham Kaplan, *The Conduct of Inquiry: Methodology for Behavioral Science* (San Francisco: Chandler Publishing Company, 1964), pp. 259-262. Allan Nevins, *The Gateway to History* (Boston: D. C. Heath and Company, 1938), pp. 240-250, lists seven general philosophies of history.

[50] Heidbreder, *Seven Psychologies*, p. 413.

Chapter 4

[1] Ernest C. Richardson, *Classification: Theoretical and Practical,* 3d ed., (Hamden, Conn.: Shoe String Press, Inc., 1964), pp. 48-49.

[2] Ibid.

[3] Boyer, *History of Mathematics*, p. 8.

[4] Richardson, *Classification*, p. 51.

[5] Conrad H. Rawski, "The Interdisciplinarity of Librarianship," in *Toward a Theory of Librarianship*, ed. by Conrad H. Rawski (New York: Scarecrow Press, 1972).

[6] Cherry, *On Human Communication*, p. 6.

[7] Shiyali R. Ranganathan, *Prolegomena to Library Classification* (London: The Library Association, 1957), pp. 125-137.

[8] Ibid., p. 391.

[9] Quoted in Ian M. L. Hunter, *Memory* (Baltimore: Penquin Books, 1964), p. 66.

[10] See, for example, Appendix iv, "Tables of Earned Doctorates," (Humanities, Biological Sciences, Physical Sciences, Social Sciences) in Allan M. Cartter, *American Colleges and Universities* (Washington, D. C.: American Council on Education, 1964), pp. 1260-1278. Academic divisions of the University of California at Los Angeles and the University of Chicago are based on these four broad areas.

[11] Sources: Conrad H. Rawski, "Bibliographic Organi-

zation in the Humanities," *Wilson Library Bulletin* XL (April 1966), 740-744; William G. Pollard, "Physical Science," *McGraw-Hill Encyclopedia of Science and Technology*, 1st ed., X, 207-208; Charles B. Curtin, "Biology," Ibid., II, 219-220; Bert F. Hoselitz, ed., *A Reader's Guide to the Social Sciences* (Glencoe, Ill.: Free Press, 1959), p. 5. The areas in the biological sciences are common to both zoology and botany.

[12] Bert F. Hoselitz, "The Social Sciences in the Last Two Hundred Years," in *Reader's Guide to the Social Sciences*, ed. by Hoselitz, pp. 7-9, 15.

[13] Talcott Parsons, "Unity and Diversity in the Modern Intellectual Disciplines: the Role of the Social Sciences," *Daedalus* 94 (Winter 1965), pp. 39-65.

[14] Price, *Science Since Babylon*, p. 116.

[15] Ibid., p. 117.

[16] L. L. Bernard, "The Social Sciences as Disciplines: United States," *Encyclopedia of Social Sciences*, I, 332.

[17] Ibid.

[18] Ibid., pp. 341-342.

[19] John Dewey, "Unity of Science as a Social Problem," *International Encyclopedia of Unified Sciences*, I, 32-33.

[20] See, for example, Walter J. Ong, "Crisis and Understanding in the Humanities," *Daedalus* 98 (Summer 1969), 617-640; Parsons, "Unity and Diversity in the Modern Intellectual Disciplines," *Daedalus* 94 (Winter 1965), 40-43.

[21] Vannevar Bush, *Science Is Not Enough* (New York: William Morrow and Company, 1967), p. 28.

[22] Floyd W. Matson, *The Broken Image* (Garden City, N. Y.: Doubleday and Company, 1966), pp. 3-29.

[23] R. G. H. Siu, *The Tao of Science: An Essay on Western Knowledge and Eastern Wisdom* (Cambridge, Mass: M. I. T. Press, 1957), p. 160.

[24] William T. Jones, *The Sciences and the Humanities: Conflict and Reconciliation* (Berkeley: University of California Press, 1965), pp. 5, 222.

[25] Bell, *Development of Mathematics*, p. 594, briefly discusses the future possibility of mysticism in mathematics.

[26] Randal L. Dahling, "Shannon's Information Theory: The Spread for an Idea," *Studies of Innovation and of Communication to the Public* (Stanford: Institute for Communication Research, Stanford University, 1962), pp. 119-136.

[27] Ludwig von Bertalanffy, *General Systems Theory: Foundations, Development, Applications* (New York: George Braziller, 1968), p. 14.

[28] Don R. Bowen, *Political Behavior of the American Public* (Columbus, Ohio: Charles E. Merrill Publishing Company, 1968), p. 3; Oran R. Young, *Systems of Political Science* (Englewood Cliffs, N. J.: Prentice-Hall, Inc., 1968), pp. 13-48.

[29] "Classification Research Group Bulletin No. 8," *Journal of Documentation* 20 (September 1964), 158.

[30] Bonifati M. Kedrov, "Sur la classification des sciences," in *Proceedings of the Second International Congress of the Unity of the Sciences: Zurich, 1954,* Vol. I: *Plenary Sessions* (Neuchatel Suisse: Editions du Griffon, 1955), pp. 68, 76.

[31] Peter Caws, "Science and System," *General Systems,* Thirteenth Yearbook, p. 5.

[32] The following account is based on my paper, "The World Encyclopedia as a General System of Models," to be published in Conrad H. Rawski, ed., *Toward a Theory of Librarianship* (New York: Scarecrow Press, 1972).

[33] Arthur C. Clarke, *Profiles of the Future* (New York: Bantam Books, Inc., 1962), p. 235.

[34] H. G. Wells, *World Brain* (Garden City, N. Y.: Doubleday, Doran and Co., Inc., 1938), pp. 7, 35.

[35] Ibid., pp. 22-23, 28.

[36] Kenneth E. Boulding, *The Image: Knowledge in Life and Society* (Ann Arbor: University of Michigan Press, 1956), p. 164.

[37] Harold D. Lasswell, "Strategies of Inquiry: The Rational Use of Observation," in *The Human Meaning of the*

Social Sciences, ed. by Daniel Lerner (Cleveland: World Publishing Company, 1959), pp. 89-113.

[38] Paul Weiss, "Knowledge: a Growth Process," *Science* 124 (June 10, 1960), 1716-1719.

[39] C. West Churchman, "Toward a Mathematics of Social Science: A World Information Center," in *Mathematical Explorations in Behavioral Science,* ed. by Fred Massarik and Philburn Ratoosh (Homewood, Ill.: Richard D. Irwin, Inc., and Dorsey Press, 1965), pp. 29-36.

[40] Alfred de Grazia, "The Universal Reference System," *The American Behavioral Scientist* 8 (April 1965), pp. 3-14; Watson Davie, "The Universal Brain: Is Centralized Storage and Retrieval of all Knowledge Possible, Feasible or Desirable?" in *The Growth of Knowledge,* ed. by Manfred Kochen (New York: John Wiley and Sons, Inc., 1967), pp. 60-65.

[41] Karl W. Deutsch, "On Theories, Taxonomies, and Models as Communication Codes for Organizing Information," *Behavioral Science* 11 (January 1966), pp. 1-17.

[42] Von Bertalanffy, *General Systems Theory,* p. 48.

[43] Boulding, "General Systems Theory," *General Systems,* First Yearbook, p. 17.

[44] Richard Levins, "Mathematical Models," *McGraw-Hill Yearbook of Science and Technology* (New York; McGraw-Hill Book Company, 1967), pp. 62-65.

[45] William Goffman and Vaun A. Newill, "Generalization of Epidemic Theory," *Nature* 204 (October 1964), 228.

[46] In Edward B. Montgomery, ed., *The Foundations of Access to Knowledge* (Syracuse, N. Y.: School of Library Science, Syracuse University, 1968), pp. 27, 31.

[47] Oliver L. Reiser, *The Integration of Human Knowledge* (Boston: Porter Sargent Publisher, 1958), pp. 389-392.

Chapter 5

[1] S. C. Bradford, *Documentation* (London: Crosby Lockwood and Sons, Ltd., 1948), pp. 9-10.

[2] Foster E. Mohrhardt, "Documentation: a Synthetic Science," *Wilson Library Bulletin* 38 (May 1964), 746. Bush and Bradford added to chronology.

[3] Vannevar Bush, "As We May Think," *Atlantic Monthly* 174 (July 1945), 101-108; Bradford, *Documentation.*

[4] U. S., National Science Foundation, Office of Scientific Information, *Current Research and Development in Scientific Documentation* (Washington, D. C.: Government Printing Office, 1957-), Nos. 1 (1957), 3 (1959) and 14 (1966); see introductions.

[5] Mohrhardt, "Documentation," p. 747.

[6] Robert A. Fairthorne, *Towards Information Retrieval* (London: Butterworth, 1961), p. 136.

[7] Brian C. Vickery, *On Retrieval System Theory* (London: Butterworth, 1961), p. 5.

[8] Joseph Becker and Robert M. Hayes, *Information Storage and Retrieval: Tools, Elements, Theories* (New York: John Wiley and Sons, Inc., 1963), pp. 431-432.

[9] Harold Borko and Lauren B. Doyle, "The Changing Horizon of Information Storage and Retrieval," *The American Behavioral Scientist* 7 (June 1964), 3.

[10] Cherry, *On Human Communication,* p. 2.

[11] "The ABS Program," *The American Behavioral Scientist* 7 (November 1964), 60.

[12] Dahling, "Shannon's Information Theory," *Studies of Innovation,* pp. 119, 136.

[13] Borko and Doyle, "Changing Horizon," *American Behavioral Scientist,* p. 4.

[14] Boulding, "General Systems Theory," *General Systems,* First Yearbook, p. 1.

[15] Samuel Kotz, *Russian-English Dictionary and Reader in the Cybernetical Sciences* (New York: Academic Press, 1966), vii-viii, xi-xiv.

[16] Carlos A. Cuadra, "Introduction to the ADI Annual Review," American Documentation Institute, *Annual Review of Information Science and Technology*, ed. by Carlos A. Cuadra, Vol. 1 (New York: John Wiley and Sons, Inc., 1966), p. 19.

[17] Ronald E. Wyllys, *Is Information Retrieval Now an Established Scientific Discipline?*, Report No. SP-1735, October, 1964 (Santa Monica, Calif.: Systems Development Corporation, 1964), p. 8.

[18] Harold Wooster, *Implications of Basic Research in Information Sciences to Machine Documentation*, Report No. AFORS-492 (Washington, D. C.: Air Force Office of Scientific Research, 1962), pp. 1-4.

[19] Harold Wooster, *Information Technology and the Information Sciences: With Forks and Hopes*, Project 9769 (Washington, D. C.: Air Force Office of Scientific Research, 1964), pp. 1-21.

[20] Air Force Office of Scientific Research, *Information Sciences: 1967*, AFOSR 68-0006 (Arlington, Va.: Air Force Office of Scientific Research, 1967), iii-vi.

[21] Robert S. Taylor, "The Information Sciences," *Library Journal* 88 (November 1, 1963), 4162.

[22] Thomas R. Prince, *Information Systems for Management Planning and Control* (Homewood, Ill.: Richard D. Irwin, Inc., 1966), Part I.

[23] Herman M. Weisman, "Information and the Discipline of Communication Sciences," *Proceedings of the American Documentation Institute: Annual Meeting, 1967* (London: Academic Press, 1967), p. 11.

[24] Ibid., pp. 11-12.

[25] Saul Gorn, "The Computer and Information Sciences and the Community of Disciplines," *Behavioral Science* 12 (November 1967), 433.

[26] Ibid.

[27] Von Bertalanffy, *General Systems Theory,* p. 86.

[28] Gorn, "Computer and Information Sciences," *Behavioral Science,* p. 448.

[29] Ibid., p. 441.

[30] Ibid., p. 439.

[31] Ibid., p. 445.

[32] Vladimir Slamecka, "Graduate Programs in Information Science at the Georgia Institute of Technology," *Special Libraries* 59 (April 1968), 248.

[33] Manfred Kochen, "Stability in the Growth of Knowledge," *American Documentation* 20 (July 1969), p. 195.

[34] Ibid., p. 188.

[35] Tosio Kitagawa, *Information Science and Its Connection with Statistics* (Fukuoka, Japan: Research Institute of Fundamental Information Science, Kyushu, University, 1968), p. 1.

[36] Ibid., pp. 11-13.

[37] Gorn, "Computer and Information Sciences," *Behavioral Science,* p. 443.

[38] Ibid., pp. 445-446.

[39] Kitagawa, *Information and Science,* p. 22.

[40] Arthur H. Bayfield, "Report of the Executive Officer: 1968: Shall Psychology 'Manage' Its Future?" *American Psychologist* 23 (December 1968), p. 845.

[41] Ibid.

[42] Becker and Hayes, *Information Storage,* p. 256.

[43] See for example Leonard Cohan and Kenneth Craven, *Science Information Personnel* (New York: Modern Language Association, 1961), pp. 1-13.

[44] Joseph T. Tykociner, *Research as a Science: Zetetics* (Urbana, Ill.: Electrical Engineering Research Laboratory, University of Illinois, 1959), p. 13.

[45] Alexander G. Hoshovsky and Robert J. Massey, "Information Science: Its Ends, Means, and Opportunities," *Proceedings of The American Society for Information Science:*

Information Transfer (New York: Greenwood Publishing Corporation, 1968), p. 48.

[46] Hunter, *Memory,* p. 65.

Chapter 6

[1] Von Laue, *History of Physics,* p. 1.

[2] Hardin, *Biology,* p. 637.

[3] David Easton, *A Framework for Political Analysis* (Englewood Cliffs, N. J.: Prentice-Hall, Inc., 1965), p. 33.

[4] Dennis F. Fisher, *Short Term Memory: an Annotated Bibliography* (Aberdeen Proving Ground, Maryland: U. S. Army Human Engineering Laboratories, 1968), p. 1; see also Supplement I, 1969. Six hundred works on short-term memory are reviewed.

[5] George A. Miller, *The Psychology of Communication: Seven Essays* (New York: Basic Books, Inc., 1967), pp. 5-13.

[6] Karl W. Deutsch, "On Theories, Taxonomies and Models as Communication Codes for Organizing Information," *Behavioral Science* 1 (January 1966), 14.

[7] James G. Miller, "Living Systems: Cross Level Hypotheses," *Behavioral Science* 10 (October 1965), 386-394.

[8] E. Wainright Martin, *Electronic Data Processing: an Introduction,* rev. ed. (Homewood, Ill.: Richard D. Irwin, Inc., 1965), pp. 103-111.

[9] Thomas S. Kuhn, *The Structure of Scientific Revolutions,* 2d ed. (Chicago: The University of Chicago Press, 1970), p. 24.

[10] Ibid., p. 181.

[11] William Goffman and Glynn Harmon, "Mathematical Approach to the Prediction of Scientific Discovery," *Nature* 229 (January 8, 1971), 103-104.

Bibliography

Books

Air Force Office of Scientific Research. *Information Sciences: 1967* AFOSR 68-0006. Arlington, Va.: Air Force Office of Scientific Research 1967.

Ball, W. W. Rouse. *A Primer of the History of Mathematics.* London: Macmillan and Co., Limited, 1927.

———. *A Short Account of the History of Mathematics.* Cambridge: Cambridge University Press, 1888.

Barnes, Harry E. *A History of Historical Writing.* Norman: University of Oklahoma Press, 1937.

Becker, Joseph and Robert M. Hayes. *Information Storage and Retrieval: Tools, Elements, Theories.* New York: John Wiley and Sons, Inc., 1963.

Bell, Eric T. *The Development of Mathematics.* New York: McGraw-Hill Book Company, Inc., 1945.

Bentley, John E. *Philosophy: an Outline-History.* Totowa, New Jersey: Littlefield Adams and Co., 1967.

Bernard, L. L. "The Social Sciences as Disciplines: United States." *Encyclopedia of Social Sciences,* Vol. I.

Bertalanffy, Ludwig von. *General Systems Theory: Foundations, Development, Applications.* New York: George Braziller, 1968.

Blass, Gerhard A. *Theoretical Physics.* New York: Appleton-Century-Crofts, 1962.

Bohr, Niels. *Atomic Physics and Human Knowledge.* New York: Science Editions, Inc., 1961.

Boring, Edward G. *A History of Experimental Psychology.* 2d ed. New York: Appleton-Century-Crofts, Inc., 1951.

Boulding, Kenneth E. "General Systems Theory - The Skeleton of Science." *General Systems.* First Yearbook of the Society for General Systems Research. Ann Arbor, Mich.: Society for General Systems Research. 1956.

————. *The Image: Knowledge in Life and Society.* Ann Arbor: University of Michigan Press, 1956.

Bowen, Don R. *Political Behavior of the American Public.* Columbus, Ohio: Charles E. Merrill Publishing Company, 1968.

Boyer, Carl B. *A History of Mathematics.* New York: John Wiley and Sons, Inc., 1968.

Bradford, S. C. *Documentation.* London: Crosby Lockwood and Sons, Ltd., 1948.

Bush, Vannevar. *Science Is Not Enough.* New York: William Morrow and Company, 1967.

Cajori, Florian. *A History of Physics.* Rev. ed. New York: Dover Publications, Inc., 1929.

Caws, Peter. "Science and System: On the Unity and Diversity of Scientific Theory." *General Systems.* Thirteenth Yearbook of the Society of General Systems Research. Ann Arbor, Mich.: Society of General Systems Research. 1968.

Cherry, Colin, ed. *Information Theory: Proceedings of the Fourth London Symposium on Information Theory, 1960.* Washington: Butterworth, 1961.

Cherry, Colin. *On Human Communication.* New York: John Wiley and Sons, Inc., 1957.

Churchman, C. West. "Toward a Mathematics of Social Science: A World Information Center. Edited by Fred Massarik and Philburn Ratoosh. *Mathematical Explorations in Behavioral Science.* Homewood, Ill.: Richard D. Irwin, Inc., and Dorsey Press, 1965.

Clarke, Arthur C. *Profiles in the Future.* New York: Bantam Books, Inc., 1962.

Cohan, Leonard and Craven, Kenneth. *Science Information, Personnel.* New York: Modern Language Association, 1961.

Collison, Robert. *Encyclopedias: Their History Throughout the Ages.* New York: Hafner Publishing Company, 1964.

Cuadra, Carlos A. "Introduction to the ADI Annual Review," American Documentation Institute, *Annual Review of Information Science and Technology.* Edited by Carlos A. Cuadra. Vol. I. New York: John Wiley and Sons, 1966.

Curtin, Charles B. "Biology," *McGraw Hill Encyclopedia of Science and Technology.* 1st ed. Vol. II.

Dahling, Randal L. "Shannon's Information Theory: The Spread of an Idea." *Studies of Innovation and of Communication to the Public.* Stanford: Institute for Communication Research, Stanford University, 1962.

Davis, Watson. "The Universal Brain: Is Centralized Storage and Retrieval of All Knowledge Possible, Feasible or Desirable?" *The Growth of Knowledge.* Edited by Manfred Kochen. New York: John Wiley and Sons, Inc., 1967.

Dewey, John. "Unity of Science as a Social Problem." *International Encyclopedia of Unified Science.* Vol. I.

Easton, David. *A Framework for Political Analysis.* Englewood Cliffs, N. J.: Prentice-Hall, Inc., 1965.

Ebbinghaus, Hermann. *Memory: A Contribution to Experimental Psychology.* Translated by Henry A. Ruger. New York: Teachers College, Columbia University, 1913.

Eves, Howard, *An Introduction to the History of Mathematics.* New York: Rinehart and Company, Inc., 1953.

Fairthorne, Robert A. *Towards Informational Retrieval.* London: Butterworth, 1961.

Fisher, Dennis F. *Short Term Memory: An Annotated Bibliography.* Aberdeen Proving Ground, Maryland: U. S. Army Human Engineering Laboratories, 1968.

Hadamard, Jacques. *The Psychology of Invention in the*

Mathematical Field. New York: Dover Publications, Inc., 1945.

Handy, Rollo and Kurtz, Paul, eds. *A Current Appraisal of the Behavioral Sciences*. Great Barrington, Mass.: Behavioral Research Council, 1964.

Hardin, Garrett. *Biology: Its Principles and Implications*. 2d ed. San Francisco: W. H. Freeman and Company, 1966.

Harmon, Glynn. "The World Encyclopedia as a General System of Models." *Toward a Theory of Librarianship*. Edited by Conrad H. Rawski. New York: Scarecrow Press, 1972.

Hart, Hornell. "Social Theory and Social Change." *Symposium of Sociological Theory*. Edited by Llewellyn Gross. Evanston, Ill.: Row, Peterson and Company, 1959.

Harvey-Gibson, R. J. *Two Thousand Years of Science*. New York: The Macmillan Company, 1931.

Heidbreder, Edna. *Seven Psychologies*. New York: Appleton-Century-Crofts, Inc., 1933.

Hoselitz, Bert F. "The Social Sciences in the Last Two Hundred Years." *Reader's Guide to the Social Sciences*. Edited by Bert F. Hoselitz. Glencoe, Ill.: The Free Press, 1959.

Hoshovsky, Alexander G. and Massey, Robert J. "Information Science: Its Ends, Means and Opportunities." *Proceedings of The American Society for Information Science: Information Trnasfer*. New York: Greenwood Publishing Company, 1968.

Hunter, Ian M. L. *Memory*. Baltimore: Penguin Books, 1964.

James, Glenn. *The Tree of Mathematics*. Arroyo Grande, Calif.: Digest Press, 1957.

Jones, William T. *The Sciences and the Humanities: Conflict and Reconciliation*. Berkeley: University of California Press, 1965.

Kaplan, Abraham. *The Conduct of Inquiry: Methodology for*

Behavioral Science. San Francisco: Chandler Publishing Company, 1964.

Kedrov, Bonifari M. "Sur la classification des sciences." *Proceedings of the Second International Congress of the Unity of the Sciences: Zurich, 1954.* Vol. I: *Plenary Sessions.* Neuchatel Suisse: Editions du Griffon, 1955.

Kelly, George A. The Psychology of Personal Constructs. Vol. I: *A Theory of Personality.* New York: W. W. Norton and Company, Inc., 1955.

Kitagawa, Tosio. *Information Science and Its Connection with Statistics.* Fukuoka, Japan: Research Institute of Fundamental Information Science, Kyushu University, 1968.

Korzybski, Alfred. *Science and Sanity.* 4th ed. Lakeville, Conn.: International Non-Aristotelian Library Publishing Company, 1958.

Kotz, Samuel. *Russian-English Dictionary and Reader in the Cybernetical Sciences.* New York: Academic Press, 1966.

Kuhn, Thomas S. *The Structure of Scientific Revolutions.* 2d ed. Chicago: University of Chicago Press, 1970.

Lasswell, Harold D. "Strategies of Inquiry: The Rational Use of Observation." *The Human Meaning of the Social Sciences.* Edited by Daniel Lerner. Cleveland: World Publishing Company, 1959.

Laue, Max Von. *History of Physics.* New York: Academic Press, Inc., 1950.

Levins, Richard. "Mathematical Models." *McGraw-Hill Yearbook of Science and Technology.* New York: McGraw-Hill Book Company, 1967.

Martin, E. Wainright. *Electronic Data Processing: An Introduction.* Homewood, Ill.: Richard D. Irwin, Inc., 1965.

Matson, Floyd W. *The Broken Image: Man, Science, and Society.* Garden City, New York: Doubleday and Company, Inc., 1964.

McCormick. W. Wallace. *Fundamentals of College Physics.* New York: The Macmillan Company, 1965.

McKenzie, A. E. E. *The Major Achievements of Science.* Vol. I. Cambridge: Cambridge University Press, 1960.

Mendenhall, William. *Introduction to Probability and Statistics.* 2d ed. Belmont, Calif.: Wadsworth Publishing Company, Inc., 1967.

Miller, George A. *The Psychology of Communication: Seven Essays.* New York: Basic Books, Inc., 1967.

Montgomery, Edward B., ed. *The Foundations of Access to Knowledge.* Syracuse, N. Y.: School of Library Science, Syracuse University, 1968.

More, Louis T. *Isaac Newton: A Biography.* New York: Scribner's Sons, Inc., 1934.

Neuman, John von. *The Computer and the Brain.* New Haven, Conn.: Yale University Press, 1958.

Nevins, Allan. *The Gateway to History.* Boston: D. C. Heath and Company, 1938.

Newell, Allen and Simon, Herbert A. "Overview: Memory and Process in Concept Formation." *Concepts and the Structure of Memory.* Edited by Benjamin Kleinmuntz. New York: John Wiley and Sons, Inc., 1966.

Parsons, Talcott and Shils, Edward A., eds. *Toward a General Theory of Action.* Cambridge, Mass.: Harvard University Press, 1951.

Pauli, Wolfgang. "Exclusion Principle and Quantum Mechanics." Nobel Foundation, *Nobel Lectures: Physics 1942-1962.* Amsterdam, Netherlands: Elsevier Publishing Company, 1964.

Piaget, Jean. *On the Development of Memory and Identity.* Worcester: Clark University Press, 1967.

Poincaré, Henri. "Mathematical Creation." *The Creative Process.* Edited by Brewster Ghislin. Berkeley: University of California Press, 1952.

Pollard, William G. "Physical Sciences." *McGraw-Hill Encyclopedia of Science and Technology.* 1st ed. Vol. X.

Price, Derek J. de Solla. *Little Science, Big Science.* New York: Columbia University Press, 1963.

————. *Science Since Babylon.* New Haven, Conn.: Yale University Press, 1961.

Prince, Thomas R. *Information Systems for Mangaement Planning and Control.* Homewood, Ill.: Richard D. Irwin, Inc., 1966.

Ranganathan, Shiyali R. *Prolegomena to Library Classification.* London: The Library Association, 1957.

Rawski, Conrad H. "The Interdisciplinarity of Librarianship." *Toward a Theory of Librarianship.* Edited by Conrad H. Rawski. New York: Scarecrow Press, 1972.

Reiser, Oliver L. *The Integration of Human Knowledge.* Boston: Porter Sargent Publisher, 1958.

Reitman, Walter R. *Cognition and Thought: An Information Processing Approach.* New York: John Wiley and Sons, Inc., 1965.

Richardson, Ernest C. *Classification: Theoretical and Practical.* 3d ed. Hamden, Conn.: Shoe String Press, Inc., 1964.

Richardson, Owen W. "Thermionic Phenomena: Laws Which Govern Them." Nobel Foundation, *Nobel Lectures: Physics 1922-1941.* Amsterdam Netherlands: Elsevier Publishing Company, 1965.

Royce, Joseph R. *The Encapsulated Man.* Princeton, N. J.: D. Van Nostrand Company, Inc., 1964.

Sarton, George. *The Study of the History of Mathematics.* New York: Dover Publications, Inc., 1936.

Schlesinger, George. *Method in the Physical Sciences.* New York: The Humanities Press, 1963.

Schwartz, George and Bishop, Philip W. *Moments of Discovery.* Vol. I: *The Origins of Science.* New York: Basic Books, 1958.

Shannon, Claude E. and Weaver, Warren. *The Mathematical Theory of Communication.* Urbana: University of Illinois Press, 1949.

Shera, Jesse H. *Libraries and the Organization of Knowledge.* Hamden, Conn.: Archon Books, 1965.

Simon, Herbert A. "The Architecture of Complexity."

General Systems Tenth Yearbook of the Society for General Systems Research, Ann Arbor, Mich.: Society for General Systems Research, 1965.

————. Smithburg, Donald W., and Thompson, Victor A. *Public Administration*. New York: Alfred A. Knopf, 1959.

Singer, Charles. *A Short History of Scientific Ideas*. Oxford, England: Clarendon Press, 1959.

Siu, R. G. H. *The Tao of Science: an Essay on Western Knowledge and Eastern Wisdom*. Cambridge, Mass.: M.I.T. Press, 1957.

Smith, David E. *History of Mathematics*. Vol. I: *General Survey of the History of Mathematics*. Boston: Ginn and Company, 1925.

————. *History of Mathematics*. Vol. II. Chapter X.

Soddy, Frederick. "The Origins of the Conception of Isotopes." Nobel Foundation, *Nobel Lectures: Chemistry 1901-1921*. Amsterdam, Netherlands: Elsevier Publishing Company, 1966. © Nobel Foundation, 1922.

Struik, Dirk K. *A Concise History of Mathematics*. 3d ed. New York: Dover Publications, Inc., 1967.

Taton, René, ed. *History of Science*. Vol. II: *The Beginning of Modern Science*. New York: Basic Books, Inc., 1958.

————. *History of Science*. Vol. III: *Science in the Nineteenth Century*. New York: Basic Books, Inc., 1961.

————. *History of Science*, Vol. IV: *Science in the Twentieth Century*. New York: Basic Books, Inc., 1964.

Thayer, Lee, ed. *Communication: Concepts and Perspectives*. Washington, D. C.: Spartan Books, 1967.

Tullock, Gordon. *The Organization of Inquiry*. Durham, N. C.: Duke University Press, 1966.

Tykociner, Joseph T. *Research as a Science: Zetetics*. Urbana, Ill.: Electrical Engineering Research Laboratory, University of Illinois, 1959.

U. S., National Science Foundation, Office of Scientific

Information. *Current Research and Development in Scientific Documentation.* Washington, D. C.: Government Printing Office, 1957.

Vickery, Brian C. *On Retrieval System Theory.* London: Butterworths, 1961.

Weinberg, Alvin M. *Reflections on Big Science.* Cambridge, Mass.: M.I.T. Press, 1967.

Weisman, Herman M. "Information and the Discipline of Communication Sciences," *Proceedings of the American Documentation Institute: Annual Meeting, 1967.* London: Academic Press, 1967.

Wells, H. G. *World Brain.* Garden City, N. Y.: Doubleday, Doran and Co., Inc., 1938.

Whiteside, Derek T., ed. *The Mathematical Papers of Isaac Newton.* Vol. I: *1664-1666.* Cambridge: Cambridge University Press, 1967.

Wiener, Norbert. *I Am a Mathematician.* Garden City, New York: Doubleday and Company, 1956.

————. *The Human Use of Human Beings: Cybernetics and Society.* Garden City, New York: Doubleday and Company, Inc., 1964.

Wilder, Raymond L. *Evolution of Mathematical Concepts: An Elementary Study.* New York: John Wiley and Sons, Inc., 1968.

Wooster, Harold. *Implications of Basic Research in Information Sciences to Machine Documentation.* Report No. AFORS-492. Washington, D. C. : Air Force Office of Scientific Research, 1962.

————. *Information Technology and the Information Sciences: With Forks and Hopes.* Project 9769. Washington, D. C.: Air Force Office of Scientific Research, 1964.

Wyllys, Ronald E. *Is Information Retrieval Now an Established Scientific Discipline?* Report No. SP-1735, October, 1964. Santa Monica. Calif.: Systems Development Corporation, 1964.

Young, Oran R. *Systems of Political Science.* Englewood, New Jersey: Prentice-Hall, Inc., 1968.

———. "A Survey of General Systems Theory." *General Systems.* Ninth Yearbook of the Society for General Systems Research, Ann Arbor, Mich.: Society for General Systems Research, 1964.

Zipf, George K. *Human Behavior and the Principle of Least Effort.* Cambridge, Mass.: Addison-Wesley Press, Inc., 1949.

Periodicals

Alexander, Franz and Others. "Behavioral Science: A New Journal." *Behavioral Science* 1 (January 1956), 1-5.

Bayfield, Arthur H. "Report of the Executive Officer: 1968: Shall Psychology Manage Its Future?" *American Psychologist* 23 (December 1968), 844-848.

Borko, Harold and Doyle, Lauren B. "The Changing Horizon of Information Storage and Retrieval." *The American Behavioral Scientist* 7 (June 1968), 3-8.

Bridgman, Percy W. "Philosophical Implications of Physics." *American Academy of Arts and Sciences.* Bulletin 3 (February 1950), 136-140.

Bruner, Jerome S. "On Perceptual Readiness." *Psychological Review* 64 (May 1957), 150-153.

——— and Allport, Gordon W. "Fifty Years of Change in American Psychology." *Psychological Bulletin* 37 (December 1940), 757-776.

Bush, Vannevar. "As We May Think." *Atlantic Monthly* 174 (July 1945), 101-108.

Capek, Milic. "Ernst Mach's Biological Theory of Knowledge," *Synthese* 18 (April 1968), 171-191.

"Classification Research Group Bulletin No. 8." *Journal of Documentation* 20 (September 1964), 146-169.

Deutsch, Karl W. "On Theories, Taxonomies, and Models

as Communication Codes for Organizing Information." *Behavioral Science* 11 (January 1966), 1-17.

Goffman, William and Harmon, Glynn. "Mathematical Approach to the Prediction of Scientific Discovery," *Nature* 229 (January 8, 1971), 103-104.

————and Newill, Vaun A. "Generalization of Epidemic Theory." *Nature* 204 (October 17, 1964), 225-228.

Gorn, Saul. "The Computer and Information Sciences and the Community of Disciplines." *Behavioral Science* 12 (November 1967), 433-452.

Grazia, Alfred de. "The Universal Reference System." *The American Behavioral Scientist* 8 (April 1965), 3-14.

Kedrov, Bonafari M. "Toward a Methodological Analysis of Scientific Discoveries." *The Soviet Review* 4 (Spring 1963), 60-71.

Kochen, Manfred. "Stability in the Growth of Knowledge," *American Documentation* 20 (July 1969), 186-197.

Miller, George A. "The Magical Number Seven, Plus or Minus Two: Some Limits on Our Capacity for Processing Information." *Psychological Review* 63 (March 1956), 81-97.

Miller, James G. "Living Systems: Cross Level Hypotheses." *Behavioral Science* 10 (October 1965), 380-411.

Mohrhardt, Foster E. "Documentation: a Synthetic Science." *Wilson Library Bulletin* 38 (May 1964), 743-749.

Ong, Walter J. "Crisis and Understanding in the Humanities." *Daedalus* 98 (Summer 1969), 617-640.

Parsons, Talcott. "Unity and Diversity in the Modern Intellectual Disciplines: the Role of the Social Sciences." *Daedalus* 94 (Winter 1965), 39-65.

Rawski, Conrad H. "Bibliographic Organization in the Humanities." *Wilson Library Bulletin* 40 (April 1968), 738-750.

Slamecka, Vladimir. "Graduate Programs in Information Science at the Georgia Institute of Technology." *Special Libraries* 59 (April 1968), 246-250.

Taylor, Robert S. "The Information Sciences." *Library Journal* 88 (November 1, 1963), 4161-4163.

"The A B S Program." *American Behavioral Scientist* 8 (November 1964), 60.

Weiss, Paul. "Knowledge: a Growth Process." *Science* 131 (June 10, 1960), 1716-1719.

Yngve, Victor H. "A Model and a Hypothesis for Language Structure." *Proceedings of the American Philosophical Society* 104 (October 1960), 444-466.

Index